A CELEBRATION
OF HUMANISM
AND FREETHOUGHT

"The Fair Venetian"
by Titian
(Tiziano Vecelli, 1477-1576)

A CELEBRATION
OF HUMANISM
AND FREETHOUGHT

RICHLY ILLUSTRATED
WITH RARE ENGRAVINGS

DAVID ALLEN WILLIAMS

 Prometheus Books

59 John Glenn Drive
Amherst, New York 14228-2197

Published 1995 by Prometheus Books

99 98 97 96 95   5 4 3 2 1

Library of Congress Cataloging-in-Publication Data

A celebration of humanism and freethought / [compiled] by David Allen Williams.
    p. cm.
    Includes bibliographical references and indexes.
    ISBN 0-87975-969-0 (alk. paper)
    1. Free thought—Quotations, maxims, etc. 2. Humanism—Quotations, maxims, etc. I. Willams, David Allen.
BL2747.C45 1995   95-14141
211'.4—dc20   CIP

Printed in the United States on acid-free paper.

IN IMITATION OF THE CLASSICS
FOR
THE ARTIST OF LIFE AND READER OF DISCERNMENT

"Philosophy" was ancient humanism.
Humanism is philosophy made modern.

Tantara! Tantara! Tantara![1]

---

1. Tantara, the sound of trumpets. "Renown," an engraving from a sculpture by Marius Jean Antonin Mercie (1845–1916).

O' MODERN READER

From the beginning, there were only two systems as guides to the higher life. The one was religion and the other was philosophy (what moderns call "humanism"). And so it is today. Here you will sample the intellect, the wit, and beauty of the ages.

PHILOSOPHY

This Medicine for the Soul
and
The Great Consolation

Saith Philosophy:
Man was not born to believe,
but to strive to understand.

"Art and Literature"
by William Bouguereau

DEAR HONORED GUEST

As a curious believer or lifelong skeptic, welcome to A *Celebration of Humanism and Freethought*. At our celebration, many great philosophers will speak, but the guests are not limited by the title of my book. Poets, as well as artists, will also make presentations. We celebrate, after all, not only philosophy, but also the universe of the good and the beautiful. And how can there be a celebration without some good old-fashioned fun?—as in "Washing Venus" (p. 192). Further, as a collector of old books, I have included some of the rare engravings for the simple reason that they deserve to see the light of day after a hundred years of being lost in many a dusty volume. They are for enjoyment only, not as proof of philosophical points. The same is true of some of the written selections. I make no claim that they were all written by "humanists." A couple of selections, in fact, appear only as historical curiosities, such as "No Baths For Virgins" (p. 86). Forgive me, St. Jerome!

This is a celebration for browsers, and each pair of facing pages is designed to stand alone. Except for the order of putting first things first, we will skip back and forth through the centuries. In general, and scorning consistency, on the left-hand page you will find commentary about the quotation or rare engraving on the right-hand page. (The quotations are set off from my commentary by the usual quotation marks or, in the case of extended excerpts, by a smaller typeface.) Notes to the quotations and illustrations begin on p. 269, and the index is on p. 299f. As for my meditations on "virtue, nobility, and excellence," you must realize that your host is a very imperfect man. Only pride and the publisher's constraints on the length of my book prevent me from listing my sins.

And a special note to the devout: Any instance of irreverence, it is hoped, will be seen as mild, and please forgive an occasional exuberance that I would not normally make in mixed company. And now slowly, in the spirit of truth and shunning all fanaticism, let us begin.

"No Praise, then, is too great for Philosophy!"

Marcus Tullius Cicero (100–43 B.C.E.)

Virtue
Nobility
Excellence

"The length of things is vanity, only their height is joy."

George Santayana (1863–1952)

FREETHINKERS

Some ten years after writing *War and Peace* (1866), Tolstoy went through a period of questioning the purpose of life. He was then a famous and prosperous man of almost fifty, but he renounced the Russian Orthodox Church, the religion of the establishment, and evolved a new Christianity founded on Christ's words, "Resist not evil."

Historian Jesse D. Clarkson described Tolstoy's new ethical religion as an "untheological Christianity" and its founder as a crusader, champion of the oppressed, and thunderer "against alcohol and tobacco as well as against the 'immorality' of all forms of violence."

Interestingly, Tolstoy's thunder over tobacco was far from new in the world. It was preceded by distant rumblings as early as 1604 when King James published his *Counterblaste to Tobacco*. The importation of tobacco into England was banned and its use in the churches prohibited. King James's book is forgotten, but the one named in his honor—the great work completed by fifty scholars in 1611, has found eternity. And what majesty!

"In the beginning God created the heaven and the earth."

INTELLECTUAL HONESTY

Leo Tolstoy (1828–1910):

> I divide men into two lots. They are freethinkers, or they are not-freethinkers. I am not speaking of. . . . the agnostic English Freethinkers, but I am using the word in its simplest meaning. Freethinkers are those who are willing to use their minds without prejudice and without fearing to understand things that clash with their own customs, privileges, or beliefs. This state of mind is not common, but it is essential for right thinking; where it is absent, discussion is apt to become worse than useless. A man may be a Catholic, a Frenchman, or a capitalist, and yet be a freethinker; but if he put his Catholicism, his patriotism, or his interest, above his reason, and will not give the latter free play where those subjects are touched, he is not a freethinker. His mind is in bondage.

THE PHILOSOPHER

Although George Santayana was an atheist, his "essential tenderness toward the religious tradition led one wit to say aptly: 'Santayana believes that there is no God, and that Mary is His mother.'"

Born in Spain of Catholic upbringing, Santayana came to America and eventually taught philosophy at Harvard University (1889–1912) and later at universities in France and Italy. He was a poet as well as the author of innumerable brilliant and witty aphorisms. His many philosophical works include:

> *The Life of Reason* (five volumes, 1905–06)
> *Winds of Doctrine* (1913)
> *Soliloquies in England* (1922)
> *Scepticism and Animal Faith* (1923)
> *The Realm of Truth* (1937).

FANATICISM DEFINED

George Santayana:

"Fanaticism consists of redoubling your effort when you have forgotten your aim."

* * *

"To ask a man, in the satisfaction of a metaphysical passion, to forego every other good is to render him fanatical and to shut his eyes daily to the sun in order that he may see better by star-light."

Remember Your Goal.

WHAT TO AVOID

There is in all good satire a happy cynicism that should not be mistaken for bitterness that others believe differently from the way we believe. Although philosophy (or its modern equivalent, humanism) often refutes traditional religious beliefs, it is idealistic in its assumption that man can live a virtuous life and achieve social progress without the help of a god. In this sense, traditional religion is more cynical about the nature of man than philosophy.

The cynic believes that people are motivated entirely by selfishness, but this attitude is blind to history, or rather it sees only in black and white the astounding technicolor of the world stage.

Not so with Oscar Wilde, the Irish poet and dramatist, who wrote *A Picture of Dorian Gray* (1891), a novel in which a man sells his soul to the devil in exchange for youth, only to see the face in his portrait age. Wilde, who gained notoriety for his art-for-art's-sake eccentricities, was imprisoned at hard labor in 1895 for homosexual practices. Needless to say, he was not born in an age of tolerance, and yet it was Wilde, who had reason to be bitter,[1] who penned the words (opposite) for which the cynic has no answer.

---

1. Even though he was embroiled in controversy and destroyed by prison, Wilde, at least in his later years, "never bore any ill-will to anybody."

CYNICISM

Oscar Wilde (1854–1900):

"A cynic is a man who knows the price of everything and the value of nothing."

    This famous paraphrase is from the comedy "Lady Windermere's Fan" (1892), whose title refers to a "fan," as in hand-held variety. In the play, Cecil Graham asks: "What is a cynic?" To which Lord Darlington replies: "A man who knows the price of everything and the value of nothing."

The failure to see

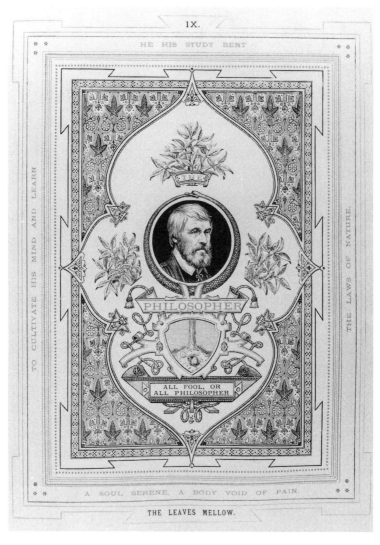

"All Fool, or All Philosopher"

The Life of Man Symbolized by the Months of the Year (London, 1866), illustrated by John Leighton. Note the details.

With favoring winds, o'er sunlit seas,
We sailed for the Hesperides,
The land where golden apples grow;
But that, ah! that was long ago.

How far, since then, the ocean streams
Have swept us from that land of dreams,
That land of fiction and of truth,
The lost Atlantis of our youth!

Whither, ah, whither? Are not these
The tempest-haunted Orcades,
Where sea-gulls scream, and breakers roar,
And wreck and sea-weed line the shore?

Utima Thule! Utmost Isle!
Here in thy harbors for a while
We lower our sails; a while we rest,
From the unending, endless quest.

Read them well, these beautiful lines by Longfellow:

"Ultima Thule," figuratively the uttermost point attainable, but also an island, perhaps Iceland, first mentioned by Pytheas, a Greek navigator of the fourth century B.C.E. Illustration from *The Poetical Works of Longfellow* (1880).

ON THINGS OF VALUE

Consider now Santayana's truth. Life cannot be built on cynicism. Philosophy is the light that leads us to the higher plane of human existence.

"The Life of Reason will then be a name for that part of experience which perceives and pursues ideals—all conduct so controlled and all sense so interpreted as to perfect natural happiness."

*   *   *

"For the Life of Reason, being the sphere of all human art, is man's imitation of divinity."

*   *   *

"That life is worth living is the most necessary of assumptions and, were it not assumed, the most impossible of conclusions."

TO CONFUSE THE INTENT
OF SATIRE

George Santayana:

> The picture of life as an eternal war for illusory ends
> was drawn at first by satirists, unhappily with too
> much justification in the facts. Some grosser minds,
> too undisciplined to have ever pursued a good either
> truly attainable or truly satisfactory, then proceeded
> to mistake that satire on human folly for a sober
> account of the whole universe.

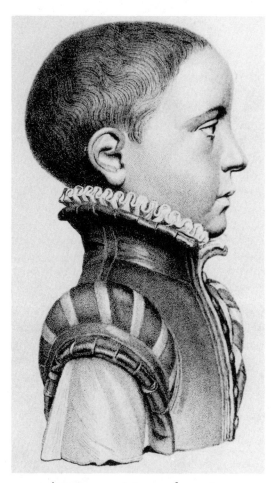

A premonition of genius

This engraving was made from a bust of Francis Bacon as a boy. As his genius matured, Bacon laid the foundation for the emergence of modern science. It was Bacon who "rang the bell that called the wits together" and announced the end of the Age of Faith and the beginning of the Age of Discovery.

"TO WEIGH AND CONSIDER"

Francis Bacon (1561–1626):

Crafty men condemn studies; simple men admire them; and wise men use them; for they teach not their own use . . . . Read not to contradict and confute; nor to believe and take for granted; nor to find talk and discourse; but to weigh and consider.

Some books are to be tasted, others to be swallowed, and some few to be chewed and digested; that is, some books are to be read only in parts; others to be read, but not curiously; and some few to be read wholly, and with diligence and attention. Some books also may be read by deputy, and extracts made of them by others; but that would be only in the less important arguments, and the meaner sort of books; else distilled books are like common distilled waters, flashy things. Reading maketh a full man, conference a ready man, and writing an exact man. And therefore if a man write little, he need have a great memory; if he confer little, he need have a present wit; and if he read little, he need have much cunning, to seem to know what [1] he doth not.

---

1. "That" has been changed to "what," and to modernize, a couple of "hads" were also dropped.

"OF MIRACLES"

If David Hume, the Scottish philosopher, had been a sculptor, what inspiring monuments to reason he might have formed out of marble. But his medium was the English language, and as his biographer, E. G. Mossner, said of the *Philosophical Essays*, they were "a work of art, polished and impersonal."

What Hume hoped to accomplish was to "shake off the yoke of authority, accustom men to think for themselves, give new hints which men of genius may carry further and, by the very opposition, illustrate points wherein no one before suspected any difficulty." And so he did! There should be a law that you may take whatever opinion you wish on miracles but first you must read Hume's short essay, "Of Miracles." Perhaps this law should be introduced in some Bible-Belt legislature!

Now to place our philosopher in perspective. Hume met Benjamin Franklin and later corresponded with him, and stepping back to the year 1760, we would find the following men.

> Thomas Jefferson, age 17
> George Washington, age 28
> David Hume, age 49
> Benjamin Franklin, age 54
> Voltaire (Francois Marie Arouet), age 66

THE QUINTESSENCE OF REASON

David Hume (1711–1776):

With what greediness are the miraculous accounts of travelers received, their descriptions of sea and land monsters, their relations of wonderful adventures, strange men and uncouth manners? But if the spirit of religion join itself to the love of wonder, there is an end of common sense, and human testimony in these circumstances loses all pretensions to authority. A religionist may be an enthusiast and imagine he sees what has no reality; he may know his narrative to be false, and yet persevere in it with the best intentions in the world, for the sake of promoting so holy a cause. Or even where this delusion has not place, vanity, excited by so strong a temptation, operates on him more powerfully than on the rest of mankind in any other circumstances; and self-interest, with equal force. His auditors may not have, and commonly have not, sufficient judgment to canvass his evidence; what judgment they have, they renounce by principle, in these sublime and mysterious subjects. Or if they were ever so willing to employ it, passion and a heated imagination disturb the regularity of its operations. Their credulity increases his impudence, and his impudence overpowers their credulity.[1]

---

1.   What a brilliant line! Now consider the words carefully. Credulity: belief and believing too readily. Impudence: being shamelessly bold.

"THE DOG OF DIOGENES GONE MAD"

Why Voltaire twice wound up imprisoned in the Bastille is hinted at in his much-later review of Jean-Jacques Rousseau's back-to-nature philosophy. "Your book makes one long to go on all fours," he said, calling Rousseau "the dog of Diogenes gone mad." (The ancient Greek Diogenes, lived like a dog, rejecting all forms of civilization. Hence comes the word "cynic," after the Greek word for dog.)

Voltaire's brilliance at satire got him into trouble from the beginning of his long life of eighty-three years. And yet, as historian Will Durant writes, "darkly as we see him through the glass of time, what a spirit!—'sheer intelligence transmuting anger into fun, fire into light.'" In his famous *Candide or Optimism*, Voltaire attacked the philosophies of Pope (an Englishman) and Leibnitz (a German), who had both championed the idea that we live in the best of all possible worlds that God could have made. But allow Mr. Pope, the eloquent poet, to speak for himself:

> All discord, harmony not understood;
> All partial evil, universal good:
> And, spite of pride, in erring reason's spite,
> One truth is clear, Whatever is, is right.

IT'S ALL FOR THE BEST!
(A REPLY TO ALEXANDER POPE)

Voltaire (1694–1778):

> [The captain of the sunken ship] was a Dutch pirate...the very same who had robbed Candide. The immense wealth this scoundrel had stolen was swallowed up with him in the sea and only a sheep was saved.
>
> "You see," said Candide to Martin, "that crime is sometimes punished; this scoundrel of a Dutch captain has met the fate he deserved."
>
> "Yes," said Martin, "But was it necessary that the other passengers on his ship should perish too? God punished the thief, and the devil punished the others."

And earlier, "I was fast asleep in bed when it pleased Heaven to send the Bulgarians to our noble castle...they murdered my father and brother and cut my mother to pieces."

Yet, Voltaire was not an atheist, even if he said that "the first divine [priest] was the first rogue who met the first fool."

LINES THAT BECAME A PART OF OUR LANGUAGE

Alexander Pope (1688–1744):

> "A little learning is a dangerous thing; Drink deep, or taste not the Pierian spring." [1]

> * * *

> "To err is human; to forgive divine."

> * * *

> "Fools rush in where angels fear to tread."

> * * *

> "Hope springs eternal in the human breast: Man never is, but always to be blessed."

> * * *

> "Know then thyself, presume not God to scan, The proper study of mankind is Man."

What a tribute to the human spirit! All this optimism from a man who was born a dwarf and handicapped. The son of a linen draper, Pope was a Catholic at a time when Catholics could neither attend universities nor hold public office. And woe to those who slighted him! For Pope, like Voltaire, was a master at satire.

---

1. In Greek mythology, the Pierian spring was the place where the Muses (the nine goddesses of literature, the arts, and the sciences) worshiped.

AND VICE VERSA

Alexander Pope (1688–1744, an English Catholic):

"An Honest Man's the noblest work of God."

Robert Ingersoll (1833–1899, American Agnostic):

"An Honest God is the noblest work of Man."

From Pope's "Essay on Man" (1733–34), and *The Gods* (1876) by Ingersoll, who also said: "A good deed is the best prayer," and "A loving life is the best religion."

O TIME!

Time

is

Too slow for those who wait,

Too swift for those who fear,

Too long for those who grieve,

Too short for those who rejoice,

But for those who love, time is

Eternity.

Hours fly,

Flowers die,

New days,

New ways,

Pass by.

Love stays.

An anonymous inscription on a sundial at the University of Virginia, Charlottesville.

"With them I take delight in weal,
And seek relief in woe."

An hourglass, some roses, and a philosopher in her library

"My days among the dead are pass'd;
Around me I behold,
Where'er these casual eyes are cast,
The mighty minds of old."

Lines by Robert Southey (1774–1843)

LOST IN "THE NEBULOUS WASTES"

It is tragic that Walter Beran Wolfe, an American psychiatrist, did not live longer and produce more such gems as are found in *How to be Happy though Human* (1931). Wisdom there is, but in the now-dated book are many instances of that unintended humor which befalls all prophecies.

"Homosexuality can be cured, and is cured daily, by competent psychiatrists....Fifty years from today homosexuality will not be looked on as a congenital anomaly, but as a form of bad manners."

Dr. Wolfe was only thirty when he wrote his book, and in all probability would have modernized his views with the changing times. But at age thirty-five, he was killed in an automobile accident in Switzerland.

Dr. Wolfe's reference to "metaphysics" (opposite) brings to mind the satire *Zadig* (1747), in which Voltaire spoke of a Babylonian philosopher, "as wise as it is possible for men to be. . . . He knew as much of metaphysics as hath ever been known in any age—that is, little or nothing at all."

Oh, Voltaire! What a pain you must have been in the side of the establishment. Yet, the study of metaphysics, or of ultimate reality, as God in religion, is a part of formal philosophy, which consists of five subjects—logic, esthetics (ideal beauty), ethics, politics (ideal social organization), and metaphysics.

"A REALLY HAPPY MAN"

W. Beran Wolfe (1900–1935):

If you observe a really happy man you will find him building a boat, writing a symphony, educating his son, growing double dahlias in his garden, or looking for dinosaur eggs in the Gobi Desert. He will not be searching for happiness as if it were a collar button that has rolled under the radiator. He will not be striving for it as if it were a goal in itself, nor will he be seeking for it among the nebulous wastes of metaphysics.

To find happiness we must seek for it in a focus outside ourselves.

Or Happy Woman, Of Course!

"THINGS WHICH ARE TOO WONDERFUL FOR ME"

The Bible (Proverbs 30:18–19, written about 350 B.C.E.):

> There be three things which are too wonderful for me, yea, four which I know not: the way of an eagle in the air; the way of a serpent upon a rock; the way of a ship in the midst of the sea; and the way of a man with a maid.

"The way of a man with a maid"

Here in a painting by William Bouguereau (1825–1905),
a French artist, is the ultimate choice "Between Love and
Riches."

A DANGEROUS THOUGHT, A DANGEROUS BOOK

The book was *On the Gods*, and the thought was that they might not exist. The man was Protagoras. "For this introduction to his book," said Diogenes Laertius,[1] speaking across seventeen centuries in words we might well ponder, "the Athenians expelled him; and they burnt his works in the marketplace, after sending round a herald to collect them from all who had copies in their possession."

And oddly amusing it is that Protagoras "invented the shoulder-pad on which porters carry their burdens . . . for he himself had been a porter." Ah, to have known such a man.

---

1. Not to be confused with Diogenes (c. 412-323 B.C.E.), the famous cynic philosopher who searched for an honest man with a lantern.

"AS TO THE GODS"

Protagoras (481–411 B.C.E.):

"As to the gods, I have no means of knowing either that they exist or that they do not exist. For many are the obstacles that impede knowledge, both the obscurity of the question and the shortness of human life." [1]

Thucydides (c. 471–400 B.C.E.) expressed a similar thought on the plague in Athens: "As for the gods, it seemed to be the same thing whether one worshipped them or not, when one saw the good and the bad dying indiscriminately."

---

1. What we know of Protagoras is largely found in *Lives of Eminent Philosophers*, by Diogenes Laertius.

DIOGENES LAERTIUS

Herbert S. Long, in his introduction to *Lives of Eminent Philosophers*, said of Diogenes Laertius: "The tone of his work as a whole suits better a man of the world who happened to be interested in philosophers, but more as men and writers than as philosophers in a technical sense. If he gives a full account of Sceptic doctrines and carries the succession of that school later than of any other, it is probably because he enjoyed juggling paradoxes, the more outrageous the better."

Diogenes Laertius mentions five philosophers named "Diogenes." The most famous was the "Cynic" Diogenes (c. 412–323 B.C.E.), who lived in a tub to demonstrate his austerity and carried a lantern in the daytime to search for an honest man. The cynics held that virtue is the only good and condemned the rest of society for its materialistic pursuits.[1]

Although "cynic" has come to mean a person who believes that people in all their actions are motivated by selfishness, nowadays the ancient cynic belief in the supremacy of virtue does not always follow from the name.

---

1. See also p. 16.

DIOGENES ON DIOGENES

Diogenes Laertius (c. 225–250 C.E.):

On Diogenes, the cynic philosopher: "When he was sunning himself in the Craneum, Alexander (the Great) came and stood over him and said, 'Ask of me any boon you like.' To which he replied, 'Yes, stand from between me and the sun.'"

"Diogenes in His Tub"
by Jean-Leon Geromé (1824–1904), a french painter

IN THE GARDEN OF EPICURUS

The Greek Epicurus taught that the goal of man should be a life of pleasure regulated by morality, temperance, serenity, and cultural development. Yet, the great Cicero, a Roman, called Epicurus an "insignificant philosopher," in large part, undoubtedly, because Epicurus did not believe in life after death.[1] Said Cicero, "Even if I am mistaken in my belief that the soul is immortal, I make the mistake gladly, for the belief makes me happy."

We admire the honesty of Cicero, for such is the longing of the soul. Nevertheless, one can grow old waiting for the definitive answer to the question of immortality, and it must be conceded that there has been no progress in the subject since the days of the ancient Greeks. Notwithstanding modern near-death experiences, in which a "being of light" is encountered, the question of immortality still boils down to faith, and speaking of boiling, it was Aeson "whom Medea was said to have restored to youth by cutting him up and boiling him in a cauldron."[2]

---

1. Cicero, "On Old Age," an essay that Thomas Jefferson read once each year.

2. Ibid. One enthusiastic talk-show tunnel-walker even claimed that he couldn't wait to die again! This time permanently. The present writer sometimes envies this breezy view of the universe, where actual experience replaces the need for faith in an afterlife.

ON NOT FEARING DEATH

Epicurus (c. 342–270 B.C.E.):

"When we are, death is not; and when death is, we are not."

Reason cannot decide this issue; neither can faith. Still, one cannot argue with the desire for life. If wishes were fishes, I would rather wake up in a field of daises than to cease to exist. The only thing disturbing this pleasant vision is the worrisome line by Santayana: "The fact of having been born is a very bad augury for immortality."

What draws us to a work of art?

What secret depth does it touch that we cannot simply pass it by? Yet, philosophy does not dwell on the inevitable. Each morning is forever! Thus, we only pause to wonder at this image of "Death and Peace."

One is reminded of "Et ego in Arcadia," a phrase derived from a painting by Guercino (1590–1666) of some shepherds who have found a human skull with writing on it. "I too have lived in Arcady," a poignant expression of a great happiness now gone forever! Arcadia, a mountainous region of pagan Greece, was thought to be a place of ideal rustic contentment.

"The Secret"

Either there is a god or there is not a god, and either there is life after death, or there is not life after death. Philosophy, whose measures are virtue, nobility, and excellence, does not require that these questions be answered, but there is good in the discussion of the unknown.

Philosophy and religion part company when it is claimed that God requires belief in Himself and immortality to obtain eternal happiness. The doctrines and rituals, such as baptism, are nothing but vanity, compared to the true measures of men and women.

Painting by Edmund Blair Leighton (1853–1922), a British painter

"SOME MISTAKES OF MOSES"

He was famous (or infamous) for his attacks on fundamentalist Christian beliefs, and his name is still spoken with reverence by a new generation of freethinkers. A few of his books:

> *The Gods, and Other Lectures* (1876)
> *Some Mistakes of Moses* (1879)[1]
> *Why I Am An Agnostic* (1896)
> *Superstition* (1898)

The man was Robert Green Ingersoll, a lawyer and pillar of the Republican party, who had served as a colonel in the Union Army during the Civil War. One day when a reporter asked how much the books in his private library had cost, Ingersoll looked over his shelves and replied, "These books cost me the governorship of Illinois, and maybe the presidency of the United States as well." Ingersoll's skill as an orator is evident in one of his photographs, which shows a stout and powerful man with his hands on his hips, his jaw set, and his balding head turned in proud defiance.

---

1. The mistakes of Moses began with the first chapter of Genesis. By tradition, it is said that Moses was the author of the first five books of the Bible—Genesis, Exodus, Leviticus, Numbers, and Deuteronomy, which together comprise the Pentateuch (after the Greek "penta" for five and "teuchos" for book).

THE ORIGIN OF RELIGION

Robert Ingersoll (1833–1899):

"Our hope of immortality does not come from any religion, but nearly all religions come from that hope."

"The Death-bed of St. Cecilia" [1]
by Frans de Vriendt (1517–1570), a Flemish painter

---

1. Cecilia (b. 230?) suffered martyrdom, and since she both sang and played musical instruments, she is the patron saint of music.

"THOU DIED'ST IN ELD"

Protagoras was the first of the Greek sophists–teachers of rhetoric, politics, and philosophy. Some sophists became famous for their specious arguments; hence, "sophist" has come to mean a person who engages in clever and false reasoning. Because they accepted pay for their teaching and emphasized practical education, rather than higher philosophical concepts, the sophists were often looked down upon in Greek society.

In one of his books, *On the Gods*, Protagoras questioned the existence of the deities, and for that crime, he was banished from Athens.

"Protagoras, I hear it told of thee
Thou died'st in eld[1] when Athens thou didst flee."[2]

---

1. eld: old age.

2. One scholar counted "1,186 explicit references to 365 books by about 250 authors, as well as more than 350 anonymous references" in *Lives of Eminent Philosophers* by Diogenes Laertius. Thus, he has become "the chief continuous source for the history of Greek philosophy," since the vast majority of these works have been lost.

WHAT IS MAN?

Protagoras (481–411 B.C.E.):

"Man is the measure of all things: of those which are, that they are; of those which are not, that they are not."

The Cellini Salt-Cellar, by Benvenuto Cellini (1500–1571), a pupil of Michelangelo

"DARWIN'S BULLDOG"

An English biologist, famous for his defense of Darwin, this perennial agnostic's skill in debating evolution earned him the nickname "Darwin's Bulldog." The man was Thomas Henry Huxley, who complained that: "The myths of Paganism are as dead as Osiris or Zeus...but the coeval imaginations current among the rude inhabitants of Palestine...are regarded by nine-tenths of the civilized world as the authoritative standard of fact."

Yet, in Huxley's rejection of biblical literalism, there is hope for higher religion and philosophy. Fundamentalism still exists today, but not at "nine-tenths of the civilized world."

BY THE CRADLE OF HERCULES

Thomas Henry Huxley (1825–1895):

> It is true that if philosophers have suffered, their cause has been amply avenged. Extinguished theologians lie about the cradle of every science as the strangled snakes beside that of Hercules; and history records that whenever science and orthodoxy have been fairly opposed, the latter has been forced to retire from the lists, bleeding and crushed if not annihilated; scotched,[1] if not slain.

In Greek mythology, Hercules was the son of Zeus and Alcmena. Hera, the jealous wife of Zeus, sent two serpents to kill the infant Hercules, who seized the snakes and crushed them in his hands. It was Hercules who later freed Prometheus. Chained to a rock for giving fire to man, Prometheus had daily to suffer the pain of having an eagle (or vulture in some versions) eat his liver, which grew anew each night.

---

1. scotched: to maim, to put an end to, as in to scotch a rumor

"THE PREACHER"

"Ecclesiastes" comes from *koheleth* in Hebrew, meaning "the preacher." Yet, the Book of Ecclesiastes is notable for its resignation to the world—"the dead know not any thing, neither have they any more a reward, for the memory of them is forgotten." But don't be sad: "There is nothing better for a man than that he should eat and drink, and that he should make his soul enjoy good in his labour. This also I saw, that it was from the hand of God" (Ecclesiastes 9:5 and 2:24).

The object of philosophy is to place all things in perspective, and resignation has its place. But let it be remembered that happiness is our goal, and visions of our forgotten place in history, while sobering, do little to promote our goal if dwelt upon to excess. Such is the teaching of philosophy, the nemesis of despair, for it counsels that we should cultivate our gardens, as Voltaire urged in the final lines of *Candide*.

Remember also: "It is only charlatans who are certain." "Doubt is not a very agreeable state, but certainty is a ridiculous one."

Or, in the words of Oliver Wendell Holmes, Jr., "Certainty generally is illusion, and repose is not the destiny of man."

"A TIME TO EVERY PURPOSE"

The Bible (Ecclesiastes 3:1–8):

To every thing there is a season, and a time to every purpose under the heaven.

A time to be born, and a time to die: a time to plant, and a time to pluck up that which is planted:

A time to kill, and a time to heal: a time to break down, and a time to build up:

A time to weep, and a time to laugh: a time to mourn, and a time to dance:

A time to cast away stones, and a time to gather stones together: a time to embrace, and a time to refrain from embracing:

A time to get, and a time to lose: a time to keep, and a time to cast away:

A time to rend, and a time to sew: a time to keep silence, and a time to speak:

A time to love, and a time to hate: a time of war, and a time of peace.

A BOUT WITH UNITARIANISM

Coleridge is not remembered for his youthful fascination with pantisocracy,[1] nor his later defense of Trinitarianism after about a bout with Unitarianism. Nor is it particularly remembered that he became a slave to opium for the last thirty-one years of his life. What we remember is the opiate-induced vision of "Kubla Khan"—"a world of magic, not to be explained by rules," as Edith Sitwell said of "the splendors of Coleridge."

> In Xanadu did Kubla Khan
> A stately pleasure-dome decree:
> Where Alph, the sacred river, ran
> Through caverns measureless to man
>   ...Down to a sunless sea.
> So twice five miles of fertile ground
> With walls and towers were girdled round:
> And there were gardens bright with sinuous rills,
> Where blossomed many an incense-bearing tree;
> And here were forests ancient as the hills,
> Enfolding sunny spots of greenery.
> . . . .
> And close your eyes in holy dread,
> For he on honey-dew hath fed,
> And drunk the milk of Paradise.

---

1. Pantisocracy: all of equal rank, a government of all by all. Coleridge and the poet Robert Southey planned to set up a socialistic colony on the banks of the Susquehanna River in America. The idea never materialized.

"UPON A PAINTED OCEAN"

Samuel Taylor Coleridge (1772–1834):

> "The fair breeze blew, the white foam flew,
> The furrow followed free;
> We were the first that ever burst
> Into that silent sea."

*   *   *

> "As idle as a painted ship
> Upon a painted ocean."

*   *   *

> "Water, water, everywhere
> Nor any drop to drink."

And so in pleasure it all comes back. Some memory from our youth, a shaft of sunlight across our desk, the voice of a stern but lovable English teacher. "I will now read from 'The Rime of the Ancient Mariner.' Please pay close attention." Yes, Mrs. Hansen, and we always will.

Said Coleridge, "He, who begins by loving Christianity better than Truth, will proceed by loving his own Sect or Church better than Christianity, and end in loving himself better than all."

A "GUIDE TO THE PERPLEXED"

Beginning in 1935, Will Durant, and later with his wife Ariel, authored *The Story of Civilization*, a monumental work in eleven volumes. The tenth volume, *Rousseau and Revolution*, won the Pulitzer Prize in 1968. Durant is quoted here from his classic chronicle of men and ideas, *The Story of Philosophy* (1926), a book that is still in print today.

Durant is speaking of the effect of certain arguments on the philosopher Benedict Spinoza:

> He read in Maimonides a half-favorable discussion of the doctrine of Averroes,[1] that immortality is impersonal; but he found in the *Guide to the Perplexed* more perplexities than guidance. For the great Rabbi propounded more questions than he answered; and Spinoza found the contradictions and improbabilities of the Old Testament lingering in his thought long after the solutions of Maimonides had dissolved into forgetfulness.

Will Durant! How fine! And how lucky we readers are to be your friends. How wise you were! Of Spinoza's excommunication from the Amsterdam synagogue, it was nothing for: "Fate had written that Spinoza should belong to the world."

---

1. Muhammad Averroes (Ibn Rushd, 1126–1198 C.E.), a Spanish-Arabian philosopher and physician. Maimonides (Rabbi Moses ben Maimon, 1135–1204 C.E.), a Jewish philosopher who studied under Arab scholars in Spain.

"THE CLEVEREST DEFENDERS OF A FAITH"

Will Durant (1885–1981):

"The cleverest defenders of a faith are its greatest enemies; for their subtleties engender doubt and stimulate the mind."

ETERNAL HAPPINESS

Corliss Lamont (1902–1995):

"As the pious churchwarden said to a questioner: 'Of course I believe in eternal bliss, but do let us talk about something less depressing.'"

Corliss Lamont, a great modern advocate of humanism, spent a lifetime active in liberal social causes while pursuing a career as a teacher of philosophy at Cornell, Harvard, and Columbia universities.

"Do I," writes Lamont, "who know so well the length of one earthly life, really believe that this conscious self of mine is to go on existing for 500 million years and then 500 million more and so on ad infinitum?"

Yes, let us speak of pleasant things.
Of the coast of Sicily and finding romance along a country path. It is the miracle of a wish that we are there now!

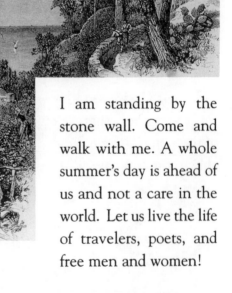

I am standing by the stone wall. Come and walk with me. A whole summer's day is ahead of us and not a care in the world. Let us live the life of travelers, poets, and free men and women!

"A DAINTY DISH EVEN FOR SPANIARDS"

Scholar and explorer Victor Wolfgang von Hagen has written extensively about ancient America, and his books belong on the list that all readers at some time or another make. Here are three of those not-to-be-missed books: *Realm of the Incas* (1957), *The Aztec: Man and Tribe* (1958), *World of the Maya* (1960). Forget the dates, Von Hagen's wit and scholarship have stood the test of time. The account of his expedition to map the 2500-mile-length of the Inca highway from Ecuador to Chile is also excellent—*The Highway of the Sun* (1955).

Von Hagen edited *The Incas of Pedro de Cieza de Leon*, a volume of that great series of books on ancient America published by the University of Oklahoma at Norman. Cieza, a Spanish chronicler of the Indians, traveled the entire length of the Inca highway a few years after the Conquest (1532).

It is to Cieza that we owe one of the first descriptions of the potato—"*earth nuts* . . . of good flavor, very acceptable to the Indians and a dainty dish even for Spaniards."

BEING ACCURATE ABOUT THE "UNKNOWABLE"

Victor Wolfgang von Hagen (1908–   ):

Cieza accepted the idea of God as furnished him by the Roman Catholic faith; he referred all to God, leaving the term in its infinite vagueness, and relying for the rest on theology, which, as we know, treats the unknowable with minutest accuracy.

It is best that we cultivate our gardens.

THE FOLLY OF TESTIMONIES

David Hume (1711–1776):

> There is not to be found, in all history, any miracle attested by a sufficient number of men of such unquestioned good sense, education, and learning as to secure us against all delusion in themselves; of such undoubted integrity as to place them beyond all suspicion of any design to deceive others; of such credit and reputation in the eyes of mankind as to have a great deal to lose in case of their being detected in any falsehood, and at the same time attesting facts performed in such a public manner and in so celebrated a part of the world as to render the detection unavoidable—all which circumstances are requisite to give us a full assurance in the testimony of men.

Or, as Pliny the Elder, remarked, "There is no occurrence so fabulously shameless that it lacks a witness." [1]

---

1. Pliny was such a lover of learning that he lingered too long to witness the eruption of Vesuvius and was killed on August 24, 79 C.E.

ON THE INVENTION OF AGNOSTICISM

Thomas H. Huxley (1825–1895):

> So I took thought and invented what I conceived to be the appropriate title of "agnostic." It came into my head as suggestively antithetic to the "gnostic" of Church history who professed to know so much about the very things of which I was ignorant . . . .
>
> *   *   *
>
> It is wrong for a man to say that he is certain of objective truth of any proposition unless he can produce evidence which logically justifies that certainty. This is what agnosticism asserts.

The *Gnostics*, members of the early Christian sect, claimed to have a special knowledge of how the divine element in human beings became separated from the spiritual sphere. It was not God who created the world with all its evils. An inferior Demiurge, opposed to spirituality, was the actual creator. Philosophy responds, "Be sober and doubt all things." [1]

---

1. Lucian of Samosata (Syria, second century C.E.) was the Mark Twain of his day. His skeptical works include *The Sale of Creeds*, *The Way to Write History*, and *The Illiterate Bibliophile*. The above line comes from *Hermotimus, or The Rival Philosophies*.

THE OTHER SIDE OF CHRISTIANITY

Thomas H. Huxley (1825–1895):

I verily believe that the great good which has been effected by Christianity has been largely counteracted by the pestilent doctrine on which all Churches have insisted, that honest disbelief in their more or less astonishing creeds is a moral offence, indeed a sin of the deepest dye, deserving and involving the same future retribution as murder and robbery. If we could only see, in one view, the torrents of hypocrisy and cruelty, the lies, the slaughter, the violations of every obligation of humanity, which have flowed from this source along the course of the history of Christian nations, our worst imaginations of Hell would pale beside the vision.

Opposite: Established to combat heresy, the Dominicans, or "Order of the Friars Preachers," were a relentless and successful foe, especially against the Albigenses, a sect named after the city of Albi in southern France. The Albigenses opposed marriage, the bearing of children, and the eating of meat. They also advocated suicide by starvation, and a miracle it is that they became so popular that a crusade had to be launched against them!

Since the Order's founding, a Dominican has always held the position of chief theologian for the papal household.

LEONELLVS SPADA BONONIENSIS
IN ECCLESIA D. DOMINICI BONONIÆ PINXIT.

"St. Dominic Burning Heretical Books"

The Spanish-born Dominic (1170–1221) founded the Dominican Order, or the "Preaching Friars." Although Dominic, himself, was peaceful, how short the step from the burning of books to the burning of men!

O' THE ANGUISH!

The price of Zedekiah's rebellion against Nebuchadnezzar II was indeed high. Jerusalem went up in flames, and Zedekiah, forced to watch as his sons were executed, was then blinded and bound "with fetters of brass" and carried off to Babylon (II Kings 25:7). Thus the Jews went into exile in 586 B.C.E.

Such is the heritage of humankind that too often our flights into the sky of ideal values are matched at other times by our descents in the abyss of cruelty. As a symbol of universal anguish, the story of Zedekiah and his sons reaches to the very core of our humanity. We cry out for justice! This cannot happen again! But it did, again and again. There is fear in the midst of our dreams of a better world; yet no list of atrocities, however long, can tarnish our idealism. The temple of philosophy will be built!

"BY THE RIVERS OF BABYLON"

The Bible (Psalms 137:1–4):

> By the rivers of Babylon, there we sat down; yea, we wept, when we remembered Zion.
>
> We hanged our harps upon the willows in the midst thereof.
>
> For there they that carried us away captive required of us a song; and they that wasted us required of us mirth, saying, Sing us one of the songs of Zion.
>
> How shall we sing the LORD's song in a strange land?

The despair, but also wonder of "The Hanging Gardens of Babylon." According to tradition, Nebuchadnezzar II built the gardens to make his new wife happy for she had been a mountain princess.

Philosophy
is
Purity
of
Reason

Like wine, mysticism in too heavy of a dose beclouds the mind. One is reminded of the words of the Roman Catholic scholar G. K. Chesterton about a "magician who turns himself into a snake or cloud: and the whole has about it that nameless note of irresponsibility." Take care with the bottle of mysticism that we do not drink too deeply and escape into some "Oneness," from which the individual cannot return.

PARABLES VERSUS DOCTRINES

George Santayana:

Parables justify themselves but dogmas call for an apologist. The genial offspring of the prophets and poets then has to be kept alive artificially by professional doctors. A thing born of fancy, moulded to express universal experience and its veritable issues, has to be hedged about by misrepresentation, sophistry, and party spirit. The very apologies and unintelligent proofs offered in its defence in a way confess its unreality, since they all strain to paint in more plausible colours what is felt to be in itself extravagant and incredible.

PANDORA

Voltaire:

> Nothing, indeed, is more spiritual and agreeable than the story of Pandora. . . . This box of Pandora, containing all the evils that have issued from it, seems to have all the charm of the most striking and delicate allusions. Nothing is more enchanting than this origin of our sufferings. But there is something still more admirable in the story of Pandora. It has a very high merit, which seems to have escaped notice; it is that no one was ever commanded to believe it.

Said Voltaire about justifying evil, "Let us return from these miserable legends to the great saying of Epicurus, which has so long alarmed the whole earth, and to which there is no answer but a sigh: 'Either God wished to prevent evil and could not do so; or he was able to do so, and did not wish."

In a 1911 edition of the *Selected Works of Voltaire*, Joseph McCabe wrote:

> He [Voltaire] did not believe in the spirituality or immortality of the soul, but he had an unshakable conviction of the existence of God. It is sometimes said that the Lisbon earthquake shook his theism. This is inaccurate. . . . He never believed that the supreme intelligence was infinite in power, and the haunting problem of evil always made him hesitate to ascribe more than limited moral attributes to his deity.

"Pandora"

by Arthur Rackham for a rare modern edition of *A Wonder Book*, by Nathaniel Hawthorne (1804–1864). This book, a retelling of Greek myths for boys and girls, was written by the author of *The Scarlet Letter* and *House of the Seven Gables*.

"FOR WHOM THE BELL TOLLS"

Poet and clergyman John Donne was raised a Catholic but later converted to the Church of England and became a popular preacher and dean of St. Paul's Church in London. Louis Untermeyer described Donne as a "deeply, even darkly, religious soul, but this did not prevent him from writing some of the most impassioned and least inhibited love poems in the English language."

In "Progresse of the Soule," an incomplete satire begun in 1601, Donne traced the soul of Eve's apple (!) through the lives of various heretics. Comment seems required, but it escapes the present writer at the moment.

"NO MAN IS AN ISLAND"

John Donne (1573–1631):

No man is an Island, intire of its selfe; every man is a peece of the Continent, a part of the maine; if a Clod bee washed away by the Sea, Europe is the lesse, as well as if a Promontorie were, as well as if a Manor of thy friends or of thine own were. Any man's death diminishes me, because I am involved in Mankind. And therefore never send to know from whom the bell tolls. It tolls for thee. [1]

---

1. These wonderful lines are from the "Devotions," and one of its phrases became the title of Hemingway's novel about the Spanish Civil War, *For Whom the Bell Tolls* (1940). The church "bell," of course, tolls at a death or funeral.

A VISION OF THE FUTURE

Tennyson's remarkable vision in "Locksley Hall" (1842) is not beyond understanding. The history of manned flight did not begin with the Wright brothers. As early as 1785, the English Channel was crossed in a hot-air balloon manned by a Jean-Pierre Blanchard, a French balloonist, and John Jeffries, an American doctor, and in 1797, the Frenchman Andre Garnerin parachuted to a safe landing after jumping from a hot-air balloon over Paris.

Undersea travel, not mentioned by Tennyson, also has a surprisingly long history. In 1620, the same year the Pilgrims came to America, a Dutch scientist demonstrated the first workable submarine, a wooden rowboat covered with treated animal hides. During the American Revolutionary War, the one-man "Turtle," powered by a hand-cranked propeller, failed in an attempt to sink a British warship in New York Harbor. In 1801, the American inventor Robert Fulton, who would build a whole line of commercial steamships, demonstrated his twenty-one foot, copper-covered "Nautilus" submarine. The name would be used by Jules Verne in his novel *Twenty-Thousand Leagues Under the Sea* (1870).

An appreciation of the technology of Tennyson's day does not in the least detract from the beauty of the poet's lines. All things are enhanced by the light of philosophy.

"ARGOSIES OF MAGIC SAILS"

Alfred, Lord Tennyson (1809–1892):

"Locksley Hall"

For I dipt into the future, far as the human eye
could see,
Saw the Vision of the world, and all the wonder
that would be;

Saw the heavens fill with commerce, argosies of
magic sails,
Pilots of the purple twilight, dropping down with
costly bales;

Heard the heavens fill with shouting, and there
rain'd a ghastly dew
From the nation's airy navies grappling in the
central blue;

Far along the world-wide whisper of the south
wind rushing warm,
With the standards of the peoples plunging thro'
the thunder-storm;

Till the war-drum throbb'd no longer, and the
battle-flags were furl'd
In the Parliament of man, the Federation of the
world.

There the common sense of most shall hold a
fretful realm in awe,
And the kindly earth shall slumber, lapt in
unversal law.

"THE CONSOLATION OF PHILOSOPHY"

Born at Rome in about 480 C.E., Anicius Manlius Severinus Boethius rose to consulship under the Gothic Emperor Theodoric the Great. Nevertheless, "Boece," as he was posthumously known in the Middle Ages, fell from favor, and he was imprisoned and eventually executed for suspicion of plotting against Gothic rule. Boethius suffered all that it is possible for a human to bear. Yet, while in prison he wrote with the "poetic artistry and philosophical brilliance" that has come down to us in *The Consolation of Philosophy*.

Although Boethius was a Catholic and believed in an afterlife, many commentators have noted his *christianisme neutralise*. This neutrality to Christianity, and absence of specific references to Christ in *Consolation* have puzzled scholars for centuries. The answer may lie in the fact that Boethius belonged "to an age in which the ancient classical culture had become assimilated to Christianity, but not absorbed by it."

Happiness, Boethius believed, comes from serenity and ridding "yourself of hope and fear." So says "Philosophy," who, in the form of a woman, appears to Boethius in the hour of his sorrow and slowly brings him to enlightenment. She is wise but also teaches some things we cannot accept today, such as "all manner of fortune is good," an idea later taken up by Alexander Pope, after the Middle Ages, that period of Christian totality unfairly described as "a thousand years without a bath."

O' PHILOSOPHY, "MY PHYSICIAN"

Boethius (c. 480–524 C.E.):

(Appearing in his cell, "Philosophy" sings to Boethius, who knows he is condemned to death.)

> Though thunderous winds resound
> And churn the seething sea,
> Hidden away in peace
> And sure of your strong-built walls,
> You will lead a life serene
> And smile at the raging storm.

I was about to write that the children of a free country are too rebellious for such resignation, and in commenting without reflection, I did not understand this lesson for a man condemned to death. Ah, as we all are! Now I understand. Oh, Philosophy. Sing to me, "my physician" and "my nurse."

"Our chief aim on this sea of life is to displease wicked men."

When "Philosophy" first appeared, Boethius was dumbfounded, and she said, "He has forgotten for a while who he is, but he will soon remember once he has recognized me." How true!

A CERTAIN WISDOM

Boethius:

> Let men compose themselves and live at peace,
> Set haughty fate beneath their feet,
> And look unmoved on fortune good and bad,
> And keep unchanging countenance:
> . . . .
> If first you rid yourself of hope and fear
> You have disarmed the tyrant's wrath.

"MY BELIEF AND UNBELIEF"

Robert Ingersoll (1833–1899):

I am an unbeliever, and I am a believer. . . . I do not believe in the "Mosaic" account of the creation, or in the flood, or the Tower of Babel, or that General Joshua turned back the sun or stopped the earth. I do not believe in the Jonah story... and I have my doubts about the broiled quails furnished in the wilderness. Neither do I believe that man is wholly depraved. I have not the least faith in the Eden, snake and apple story. Neither do I believe that God is an eternal jailer; that he is going to be the warden of an everlasting penitentiary in which the most of men are to be eternally tormented. I do not believe that any man can be justly punished or rewarded on account of his belief.

But I do believe in the nobility of human nature; I believe in love and home, and kindness and humanity; I believe in good fellowship and cheerfulness, in making wife and children happy. I believe in good nature, in giving to others all the rights that you claim for yourself. I believe in free thought, in reason, observation and experience. I believe in self-reliance and in expressing your honest thought. I have hope for the whole human race. What will happen to one, will, I hope, happen to all, and that, I hope, will be good. Above all, I believe in Liberty.

TO SEEK TRUE EXPLANATIONS

Benedict Spinoza (1632–1677):

> Those who wish to seek out the causes of miracles, and to understand the things of nature as philosophers, and not to stare at them in astonishment like fools, are soon considered heretical and impious, and proclaimed as such by those whom the mob adore as the interpreters of nature and the gods. For these men know that once ignorance is put aside, that wonderment would be taken away which is the only means by which their authority is preserved.

Said Santayana: "Spinoza is one of those great men whose eminence grows more obvious with the lapse of years. Like a mountain obscured at first by its foothills, he rises as he recedes."

> When people tell us that they have the key to all reality in their pockets, or in their hearts, that they know who made the world, and why, or know that everything is matter, or that everything is mind— then Spinoza's notion of the absolutely infinite, which includes all possibilities, may profitably arise before us. It will counsel us to say to those little gnostics, to those circumnavigators of being: I do not believe you; God is great.

Spinoza's pantheism did not admit of an afterlife.

THE PHILOSOPHER.

The man or woman

who aspires to philosophy is the most fortunate of individuals. To seize the principles of the good life, to study, to learn, to ponder, yet to be part of the world and part of humanity as a doer of good, to transcend the centuries and be in the company of the very best of men and women who have ever lived—this is our calling; this is our ideal.

"The Philosopher," by Frans Van Mieris (1635–1681), a Dutch painter

"THE WILY CALYPSO"

It is fun to remember some of Odysseus's adventures after the Trojan War. He visited the land of the Lotus-eaters, was captured along with his men by the Cyclops (whom they blinded), was a servant of the witch Circe (who turned his men into swine), and then he spent seven years on Ogygia with "the wily Calypso." Finally after twenty years, Odysseus returned home and killed the suitors of his wife, Penelope. Sadly, though, after sixteen more years, Odysseus was killed by Telemachus, his son by Circe, who committed the act not knowing that Odysseus was his father.

A traveler who ate lotus would lose all desire to return home. Tennyson set his pen to the subject in "The Lotos Eaters" (1832) with these lines as from a dream:

> they came unto a land,
> In which it seemed always afternoon.
> . . . .
>
> yellow down
> border'd with palm, and many a winding
> vale
> And meadow, set with slender galingale;[1]

---

1. galingale: the pungent, aromatic root stem of various East Indian plants of the ginger family

THE BEAUTIFUL ISLAND OF OGYGIA

Homer (between 1200 and 850 B.C.E.):

> When at last he came to that far-off island, he left
> the blue sea and passed over the land until he
> reached the great cave where Calypso lived. He
> found her in the cave, with her beautiful hair flowing
> over her shoulders. A great fire blazed on the hearth,
> and the burning logs of cedar and juniper wafted
> their fragrant scent far over the island. Calypso sat
> within by her loom, singing in a lovely voice, and
> shooting her golden shuttle to and fro. A thick cop-
> pice of trees grew round the cave, alder and aspen
> and sweet-smelling cypress. There the birds would
> sail to rest on their outspread wings, owls and falcons
> and long-tongued sea-ravens who busy themselves
> about the waters. Over the gaping mouth of the cave
> trailed a luxuriant grape-vine, with clusters of ripe
> fruit; and four rills of clear water ran in a row close
> together, winding over the ground. Beyond were soft
> meadows thick with violets and wild celery. That was
> a sight to gladden the very gods.

At the request of Athena, Zeus sent Hermes, the god
with golden winged-shoes, to demand that Calypso set
Odysseus free. Calypso was "a goddess, beautiful indeed,
but to be feared…. And yet I had the misfortune to be
brought by some power to her hearth…[for Zeus] smashed
my good ship to pieces out in the wine-dark sea."

MENELAUS.   PARIS.   DIOMEDES.   ULYSSES.   NESTOR.   ACHILLES.   AGAMEMNON.

The heroes of the Trojan War

After the war to recover the beautiful Helen, Ulysses (Odysseus, center) had a series of wonderful adventures as recorded in the *Odyssey*. The story of the Trojan War is told in the *Iliad*.

The heroes of the Trojan War are pictured above: Menelaus, Paris, Diomedes, Ulysses, Nestor, Achilles, and Agamemnon. In the poem *Doctor Faustus* by Christopher Marlowe (1564–1593), Mephostophilis conjured up a vision of Helen of Troy. In seeing her, Dr. Faustus says:

> "Was this the face that launch'd a thousand ships,
> And burnt the topless towers of Ilium? [1]
> Sweet Helen, make me immortal with a kiss."

---

1. Ilium was Troy, hence Homer's *Iliad*.

"The Judgment of Paris"

Paris chose Aphrodite as the most beautiful goddess, and his reward was the most beautiful woman in the world, Helen of Troy. Thus began the Trojan war, since Helen was already married to the king of Sparta.

Painting by Henry Peters Gray (1819–1877), an American artist

"AND NOT TO YIELD"

Alfred, Lord Tennyson:

[A selection from "Ulysses." The speaker is Ulysses (Odysseus, a hero of the Trojan War), as an old but unbroken man.]

Some work of noble note, may yet be done,
Not unbecoming men that strove with Gods.
The lights begin to twinkle from the rocks:
The long day wanes: the slow moon climbs: the deep
Moans round with many voices. Come, my friends,
'Tis not too late to seek a newer world.
Push off, and sitting well in order smite
The sounding furrows; for my purpose holds
To sail beyond the sunset, and the baths
Of all the western stars, until I die.
It may be that the gulfs will wash us down:
It may be we shall touch the Happy Isles,
And see the great Achilles, whom we knew.

Tho' much is taken, much abides; and tho'
We are not now that strength which in old days
Moved earth and heaven, that which we are, we are;—
One equal temper of heroic hearts,
Made weak by time and fate, but strong in will
To strive, to seek, to find, and not to yield.

"The Trojan Horse" by Henri Motte (1846–1922), a French painter

THE RIVER OF LIFE

Charles Algernon Swinburne (1837–1909):

> From too much love of living,
> From hope and fear set free,
> We thank with brief thanksgiving
> Whatever gods may be,
> That no life lives for ever;
> That dead men rise up never;
> That even the weariest river
> Winds somewhere safe to sea.

The Queen's "Virginal Reticence"

His thin body, waving red hair, and birdlike head caused the English poet Swinburne to be likened to "a pagan apparition at a Victorian tea party." This "brilliant but ridiculous flamingo" came "leaping onto the sleek lawn to stamp its goat foot in challenge, to deride with its screech of laughter the admirable decorum of the conversation." But even more disturbing was Swinburne's personality, which "shattered the virginal reticence of Victoria's serenest years with a book of poems."

"THERE LIVES MORE FAITH IN HONEST DOUBT"

Alfred, Lord Tennyson:

> You say, but with no touch of scorn,
>   Sweet-hearted, you, whose light-blue eyes
>   Are tender over drowning flies,
> You tell me, doubt is Devil-born.
>
> I know not: one indeed I knew
>   In many a subtle question versed,
>   Who touch'd a jarring lyre at first,
> But ever strove to make it true:
>
> Perplext in faith, but pure in deeds,
>   At last he beat his music out.
>   There lives more faith in honest doubt,
> Believe me, than in half the creeds.

Said Louis Untermeyer of the long "In Memoriam A.H.H." (1850), that it "is not only a record of his grief but a revelation of Tennyson's philosophy, the conflict of faith and doubt and final affirmation." His "final affirmation" of life:

> "Ring in the valiant man and free....
> Ring in the Christ that is to be."

"A QUAINT AND CURIOUS VOLUME"

If Edgar Allan Poe did not invent terror, he certainly re-defined its principles. Thus:

> Once upon a midnight dreary, while I pondered,
>   weak and weary,
> Over many a quaint and curious volume of for-
>   gotten lore,
> While I nodded, nearly napping, suddenly there
>   came a tapping,
> As of some one gently rapping, rapping at my
>   chamber door.
> "'Tis some visitor," I muttered, "tapping at my
>   chamber door—
>   Only this and nothing more."

And so the "Raven" comes, and with him a man of many talents—a poet as well as the author of mysteries and stories of the macabre. Edgar Allan Poe was born in Boston, and after his father disappeared and his mother died, he was adopted by John Allan of Richmond, Virginia; hence his middle name.

In his analysis of checkers (draughts) versus chess (*opposite*), Poe displayed a brilliance that makes us smile, and there is something to be gained by the careful consideration of the words he used. This selection is from *The Murders in The Rue Morgue* (1841), and it is worth reading more than once.

THE DRAUGHTS OF MR. POE

Edgar Allan Poe (1809–1849):

"The Murders in The Rue Morgue"

I am not now writing a treatise, but simply prefacing a somewhat peculiar narrative by observations very much at random; I will, therefore, take occasion to assert that the higher powers of the reflective intellect are more decidedly and more usefully tasked by the unostentatious game of draughts [checkers] than by all the elaborate frivolity of chess. In this latter, where the pieces have different and bizarre motions, with various and variable values, *what is only complex is mistaken (a not unusual error) for what is profound.* The attention here called powerfully into play. If it flag for an instant, an oversight is committed, resulting in injury or defeat. The possible moves being not only manifold but involute, the chances of such oversights are multiplied; and in nine cases out of ten it is the more concentrative rather than the more acute player who conquers. In draughts, on the contrary, where the moves are unique and have but little variation, the probabilities of inadvertence are diminished, and the mere attention being left comparatively unemployed, what advantages are obtained by either party are obtained by superior acumen.

NOSTRADAMUS, THE SAINT OF FOOLS

James Randi, a magician, lecturer, and indefatigable investigator of psychic claims, trained his skilled eyes on "Nostradamus: The Prophet for all Seasons" in an article for the *Skeptical Inquirer* (Fall 1982, cartoon below by Rob Pudim).

Nostradamus (1504–1566), a professional French prophet, predicted the past with great accuracy, but if one takes his 950 four-line "Quatrains," usually poorly translated from the French, and applies them to all of history, then the results are disappointing. As a bogus increase to the odds, the writers of sensational books often combine line pairs from different quatrains to produce a new one.

PROPHECY: HOW TO DO IT

James Randi:

(Nostradamus)

When a fish-pond that was a meadow shall be mowed,
Sagittarius being in the ascendant,
Plague, famine, death by the military hand,
The Century approaches renewal.

Now, if any event can be found in history, past, present, or yet to come that involves a war occurring near the close of a century—or an "age" of any kind—we have a "hit." Obviously it will not be difficult to find a pond (marsh, lake, pool, reservoir, aquarium, swamp, etc.) that was once a meadow (field, farm, golf course, pasture, race track, etc.) that is mowed (swept, cleared, harvested, ploughed, etc.), and it need not even be at or near the war zone in time or place. Furthermore, any war in any 90s' decade will fit, since we need not use the first two lines if we don't need them! Look in some history books and see just how many wars since the sixteenth century fall into this category.

Also, as Randi notes, "Sagittarius is 'ascendant' each and every day!"

THE GENTEEL ATHEIST

Of superstition and religion, George Santayana says with characteristic detachment and exquisite objectivity:

> For religion differs from superstition not psychologically but morally, not in its origin but in its worth. This worth, when actually felt and appreciated, becomes of course a dynamic factor and contributes like other psychological elements to the evolution of events; but being a logical harmony, a rational beauty, this worth is only appreciated by a few minds, and those least primitive and the least capable of guiding popular movements. Reason is powerless to found religions, although it is alone competent to judge them. Good religions are therefore the product of unconscious rationality, of imaginative impulses fortunately moral.
>
> Particularly does this appear in the early history of Christianity. Every shade of heresy, every kind of mixture of Christian and other elements was tried and found advocates; but after a greater or less success they all disappeared, leaving only the Church standing.

NOT FOR TOO MUCH IMAGINATION DID MEN BELIEVE

George Santayana:

"Men became superstitious not because they had too much imagination, but because they were not aware that they had any."

The Goddess Venus

"THE TEMPTATION OF SAINT ANTONY"

St. Jerome, the translator of the Bible into Latin (the Vulgate), may have had his problems in the "wilderness," but St. Antony was surely subject to more temptation—at least in art. St. Antony (c. 250–350), the founder of the first order of monks, lived as a hermit in the hills above the Nile Valley in Egypt and withstood all the wiles of the devil, and these temptations have been a favorite subject of artists ever since.

"Monk" comes from the Greek word "monos," meaning "alone." In addition to living by a "rule," Christian monks and nuns must, of course, take the vows of "poverty, chastity and obedience."

"We here only record facts; we enter into no controversy," said Voltaire after giving numerous examples of married priests in his *Philosophical Dictionary*. He mentions that after a law had been proposed at the Council of Nice (325 C.E.) commanding bishops and priests to abstain from their wives, St. Paphnutius the Martyr said, "Marriage was chastity."[1] Centuries later, Pope Gregory VII (d. 1085) became famous for excommunicating married priests.

---

1. How fine and razorlike your words, Voltaire! "We enter into no controversy," when what you really did was throw out a bunch of red meat to a pack of starving dogs.

"The Temptation of St. Antony"
by Aime Nicolas Morot (1850–1913)

NO BATHS FOR VIRGINS!

Saint Jerome (340?–420 C.E.):

> As regards the use of the bath, I know that some are
> content with saying that a Christian virgin should not
> bathe along with eunuchs or with married women,
> with the former because they are still men at heart,
> and with the latter because women with child are a
> revolting spectacle. For myself, however, I wholly dis-
> approve of baths for a virgin of full age. Such an one
> should blush and feel overcome at the idea of seeing
> herself naked. By vigils and fasts she mortifies her body
> and brings it into subjection. By a cold chastity she
> seeks to put out the flame of lust and to quench the
> hot desires of youth. And by a deliberate squalor she
> makes haste to spoil her natural good looks. Why, then,
> should she add fuel to a sleeping fire by taking baths?

My reluctance to include this extract from Jerome's
letter to Laeta was born from having been placed on the
rack of argument by G. K. Chesterton, who has devised
so many exquisite tortures for the non-Catholic. Thus:

> In short, a real knowledge of mankind will tell any-
> body that Religion is a very terrible thing; that it is
> truly a raging fire, and that Authority is often quite as
> much needed to restrain it as to impose it. Asceticism,
> or the war with the appetites, is itself an appetite. It
> can never be eliminated from among the strange
> ambitions of man. But it can be kept under some rea-
> sonable control; and it is indulged in much saner pro-
> portion under Catholic Authority than in Pagan or
> Puritan anarchy.

Only when Chesterton called the Inquisition "a dubious
experiment," did I cry to Heaven, "No!"

"Temptation"[1] is brought to you by the devil. Who else!

May we not hope that this sweet and demure maiden with the prayer-book is so fixed in religious habits that allurements to sinful pleasures are vainly presented to her? And yet, somehow, we feel a little uneasy about it. She listens to her worldly friend too willingly, and . . . we suspect the words poured into her ear are not altogether repellent.

---

1. Painting by Henri Guillaume Schlesinger, a mid-nineteenth-century German

REASON, "THE BEAUTIFUL WHORE," CRUCIFIED

Walter Kaufmann (1921–1980):

> The idea that a man must crucify his reason before he commits himself [to a philosophy or religion] is not original with Kierkegaard. There is a long Christian tradition behind it, and Luther expressed it even more powerfully than Kierkegaard. He called reason "the devil's bride," a "beautiful whore," and "God's worst enemy," and said: "There is on earth among all dangers no more dangerous thing than a richly endowed and adroit reason." Again: "Reason must be deluded, blinded, and destroyed," and "faith must trample under foot all reason, sense, and understanding."

Nevertheless, the present writer greatly admires good men and women of faith. Indeed, I admire the good and the beautiful wherever it is found. I feel no need to win every philosophical battle, for such are the urgings of fanaticism, whose devotees are led down dark paths far from the sunny fields of heaven.

Of Martin Luther, the modern Catholic scholar G. K. Chesterton said, "He was one of those great elemental barbarians, to whom it is indeed given to change the world." [1]

---

1. The non-Catholic who enters the ring with Chesterton will find himself beaten senseless and begging for the Last Rites as all his assumptions about the Middle Ages are relentlessly refuted. A must for Protestants!

Christianity is not without its faults,

as is obvious in the religious intolerance assumed by this woodcut by Lucas Cranach (1472–1533). Martin Luther is preaching the way to salvation as the pope and the Catholic clergy burn in hell.

Is it right that a virtuous person be sent to hell for having the wrong opinions about things that cannot be seen? Will a good Buddhist who rejects Christ really be damned? And doesn't justice require that the virtuous pagan stand on equal footing with the virtuous Christian in the highest levels of Heaven?

REASONABLE EXPLANATIONS

Julian Huxley (1887–1975):

> All sorts of our strangest experiences are neither supernatural nor pathological, but are natural though uncommon possibilities of the human mind. Trances, visions, or locutions, whether hallucinatory or of a type known as interior; mental ecstasy; the reproduction of marks on the skin, such as St. Francis' stigmata, by the power of suggestion; instantaneous cures of certain types of diseases by faith; the imposing of one man's will on another through suggestion, whether in or out of hypnosis; the splitting of the personality into two; automatic writing; obsessions; impulses which act with compulsive forces—all these are the strange crops which may grow from the soil of the human mind.

Thomas Henry Huxley (1825–1895), "Darwin's bulldog." Thomas's son: Leonard Huxley (1860–1933), editor and author. Leonard's sons: Julian Sorell Huxley (1887–1975), biologist and writer; Aldous Leonard Huxley (1894–1963), brother of Julian, author of *Brave New World* (1932).

"The Mesmerist"

hypnotizes Mathius, a character in *L'Illustre Docteur Math-ius* (1859), and discovers that Mathius murdered a Polish Jew. On subjects about which there is most ignorance, belief in a supernatural cause rises in proportion to igno-rance and declines in proportion to knowledge. Such is the mathematics of the soul.

"OCKHAM'S RAZOR"

William of Ockham (1300–1349):

The Theorem:
"Entities [of explanation] are not to be multiplied without necessity." [1]

Immanuel Kant (1724–1804):

The Corollary:
"The hasty appeal to the supernatural is a couch upon which the intellect slothfully reclines."

"The Law of Parsimony," or "Ockham's Razor," is in reality the first law of logic. Given two explanations, the one with the least number of assumptions is the best (and most elegant, as in mathematics). For this reason, scientific or natural explanations always carry more force in logic than those based on a supernatural premise.

This philosophical principle is named after William of Ockham (or "Occam"), known as "Doctor Invincibilis."

---

1. *Pluralitas non est ponenda sine necessitate.* Ockham, *Quodlibeta* (c. 1324).

uietly as a philosopher reads, he or she may wonder at the power of poetry and how it takes on a life of its own. Read enough and you will feel this power both inside and outside religion. Wise readers enjoy, but later remember that they have drunk from the well of desire and imagina-tion, and they should not insist that its waters be wet as the stream at their feet. After all, literal-minded and simple-mind-ed are often synonyms.

"A FREEMAN'S WORSHIP"

His essays were "perhaps the most graceful and moving presentation of the freethinker's position since the days of Hume and Voltaire," and he wrote with "courage, scrupulous logic, and lofty wisdom," as one reviewer said of Bertrand Russell's book *Why I Am Not A Christian* (1957).

This brilliant champion of humanism lived through ninety-eight years of controversy and acclaim, beginning with his contributions to mathematical logic (1903), to his opposition to England's involvement in World War I, to his being declared "unfit" in 1940 to teach philosophy at the College of the City of New York, and on to his international recognition by winning the Nobel Prize in Literature in 1950.

Bertrand Russell's spirit is probably best seen in the title of one of his most famous essays—"A Freeman's Worship." But even in his old age he was still a gadfly. "There has been a rumor in recent years to the effect that I have become less opposed to religious orthodoxy than I formerly was. This rumor is totally without foundation. I think all the great religions of the world—Buddhism, Hinduism, Christianity, Islam, and Communism—both untrue and harmful." This written in 1957 when Russell was only eighty-five.

ON THE CLASSICAL ARGUMENTS
FOR THE
EXISTENCE OF A GOD

Bertrand Russell (1872–1970):

The arguments that are used for the existence of God change their character as time goes on. They were at first hard intellectual arguments embodying certain quite definite fallacies. As we come to modern times they become less respectable intellectually and more and more affected by a moralizing vagueness.

Of course, I know the sort of intellectual arguments that I have been talking to you about are not what really moves people. What really moves people to believe in God is not any intellectual argument at all. Most people believe in God because they have been taught from early infancy to do it, and that is the main reason.

Then I think that the next most powerful reason is the wish for safety, a sort of feeling that there is a big brother who will look after you. That plays a very profound part in influencing people's desire for a belief in God.

Russell also said, "Cruel men believe in a cruel God and use their belief to excuse their cruelty. Only kindly men believe in a kindly God, and they would be kindly in any case."

MR. WELLS, THE GREAT AGNOSTIC

English agnostic and feminist Herbert George Wells wrote a thick volume called *An Outline of History* (1920), but that book, of course, is not what made him famous. His very name will always be another word for adventure— H. G. Wells! And here are some of the stories from our youth that will live forever.

> *The Time Machine* (1895)
> *The Island of Doctor Moreau* (1896)
> *The Invisible Man* (1897)
> *The War of the Worlds* (1898)

It is now a familiar story that when *War of the Worlds* was broadcast on radio in the United States on October 30, 1938, many people believed it was an actual news report and went into a panic. The voice was that of Orson Welles of the Mercury Theater of the Air. As a side light, the story is told of a Princeton geology professor who, in the midst of this cataclysmic invasion, went out at night in search of any unusual mineral specimens which the Martians might have brought with them. Such is true devotion to science!

The lesser-known novel *Tono-Bungay* (1909) reveals Wells's many talents, tinged as it is with social commentary and satire in the midst of strange voyages aboard airplanes and submarines at a time when such technologies were still underdeveloped.

"ACROSS THE GULF OF SPACE"

H. G. Wells (1866–1946):

No one would have believed in the last years of the nineteenth century that this world was being watched keenly and closely by intelligences greater than man's and yet as mortal as his own; that as men busied themselves about their various concerns they were scrutinized and studied, perhaps almost as narrowly as a man with a microscope might scrutinize the transient creatures that swarm and multiply in a drop of water. With infinite complacency men went to and fro over this globe about their little affairs, serene in their assurance of their empire over matter. It is possible that the infusoria under the microscope do the same. No one gave a thought to the older worlds of space as sources of human danger, or thought of them only to dismiss the idea of life upon them as impossible or improbable. It is curious to recall some of the mental habits of those departed days. At most, terrestrial men fancied there might be other men upon Mars, perhaps inferior to themselves and ready to welcome a missionary enterprise. Yet across the gulf of space, minds that are to our minds as ours are to those of the beasts that perish, intellects vast cool and unsympathetic, regarded this earth with envious eyes, and slowly and surely drew their plans against us. And early in the twentieth century came the great disillusionment.[1]

---

1. Wells, *The War of the Worlds* (1898). Note the date. In 1894, Percival Lowell completed his observatory in Flagstaff, Arizona, and began reporting that he saw canals on the surface of Mars.

MR. CONRAD

It is a testament to his genius that the Polish-born Joseph Conrad was relatively ignorant of English until he learned it at sea after the age of twenty. And then to become one of the greatest novelists of the English language!

As one editor said, "Although the ocean and the mysterious lands that border it are the settings for his books, the truth of human experience is his theme, depicted with vigor, rhythm and passionate contemplation of reality." Such is Conrad's power that we can travel to far-away lands by simply reading the titles to some favorite books. Now slowly and off we go.

> *Almayer's Folly* (1895)
> *An Outcast of the Islands* (1896)
> *Lord Jim* (1900)
> *The Heart of Darkness* (1902)

And let Conrad's short story "Youth" (1902) be a must read. What magnificent lines!

"O' YOUTH!"

Joseph Conrad (1857–1924):

[The speaker is "Marlow."]

And there was somewhere in me the thought: By Jove! this is a deuce of an adventure—something you read about; and it is my first voyage as second mate—and I am only twenty—and here I am lasting it out as well as any of these men, and keeping my chaps up to the mark. I was pleased. I would not have given up the experience for worlds. I had moments of exultation. Whenever the old dismantled craft pitched heavily with her counter [1] high in the air, she seemed to me to throw up, like an appeal, like a defiance, like a cry to the clouds without mercy, the words written on her stern: "Judea, London. Do or Die."

O youth! The strength of it, the faith of it, the imagination of it! To me she was not an old rattletrap carting about the world a lot of coal for a freight—to me she was the endeavor, the test, the trial of life. I think of her with pleasure, with affection, with regret—as you would think of someone dead you have loved. I shall never forget her.... Pass the bottle.

---

1. counter: the part of a ship's stern between the water line and the arched or curved part. The ship, here, was going down a great wave; hence, counter up.

"LAMENT FOR A WAVERING VIEWPOINT"

Phyllis McGinley (1905–   ):

> Ah, snug lie those that slumber
>   Beneath Conviction's roof.
> Their floors are sturdy lumber,
>   Their windows, weatherproof.
> But I sleep cold forever
>   And cold sleep all my kind,
> Born nakedly to shiver
>   In the draft from an open mind.

In her "Lament For A Wavering Viewpoint," Pulitzer Prize-winning poet Phyllis McGinley captures the heart of the liberal spirit—not "liberal" in a narrow political sense, but liberal in realizing that the universe is too large to be contained within a single doctrine, or religion, or even within philosophy, itself, for as Hamlet said (act i, v):

"There are more things in heaven and earth, Horatio, Than are dreamt of in your philosophy."

Nevertheless, philosophy is "adversity's sweet milk" (*Romeo and Juliet*, act iii, scene iii).

What pleasure, what joy in the nimble use of words!

To open a book is to rub a magic lamp and find ourselves suddenly in the company of a genii. Here he makes a poet speak her lines, there a philosopher to probe us with hard questions, and still in front of us is the world of fantasy and adventure.

And don't miss "The Fairies," by William Allingham.

> Up the airy mountain
>   down the rushy glen,
> We daren't go a-hunting
>   For fear of little men.

"THE AMERICAN THUCYDIDES"

William Hickling Prescott, "the American Thucydides," what a man! And, oh, what a gift he left humanity! *History of the Conquest of Mexico* (1843) and *History of the Conquest of Peru* (1847). To say that he was "the first American scientific historian" does him little justice.

Samuel Eliot Morison, twice winner of the Pulitzer Prize for history, wrote of Prescott, "I shall not attempt to analyze his style because it is to be enjoyed and admired, not plucked apart."

An exact wit of literary depth, Prescott refuted one writer's exaggerations by saying that he stood "with his hair on end at his own wonders."

One page later in his own words, he remarked: "The Licentiate[1] shows an appetite for the marvellous, which might excite the envy of a monk in the Middle Ages."

We smile, we admire, we wonder at this man who accomplished so much though he was half blind. Not to have read the "Conquests" of Mexico and Peru is to have missed a rare treat.

---

1. Licentiate: a person having a professional licence to practice, in this case to preach religion.

"TO AFFECT A MYSTERY"

William H. Prescott (1796–1859):

[On the Spanish and the origin of the Aztec calendar.]

> One may doubt whether, the superstition of those who invented the scheme was greater than that of those who thus impugned it. At all events, we may, without recourse to supernatural agency, find in the human heart a sufficient explanation of its origin; in that love of power, that has led the priesthood of many a faith to affect a mystery, the key to which was in their own keeping."

And speaking of the Aztec Indian, Prescott said that Ixtlilxochitl (c. 1568–1648), "lived in a state of twilight civilization, when, if miracles were not easily wrought, it was at least easy to believe in them."

THE WAY IT SHOULD HAVE BEEN

Walt Whitman (1819–1892):

> I respect Assyria, China, Teutonia, and the
> Hebrews;
> I adopt each theory, myth, god and demi-god;
> I see that the old accounts, bibles, genealogies,
> are true, without exception;
> I assert that all past days were what they should
> have been.

Of old age, Whitman said, "I see in you the estuary that enlarges and spreads itself grandly as it pours into the great sea."

Whitman was a poet of democracy but never gained wide popularity among the masses, and not until after his death was his genius fully recognized. Louis Untermeyer said of Whitman's "When Lilacs Last in the Dooryard Bloom'd," an elegy for Abraham Lincoln, that it "had to wait almost half a century before it was recognized as one of the greatest poems, and certainly the greatest elegy ever written in America."

And now to a random year—1870: Mark Twain (age 35), Robert Ingersoll (age 37), Thomas Henry Huxley (age 45), Walt Whitman (age 51). Years later, Ingersoll would speak at Whitman's funeral.

The Great Discoveries of Reason:

From apes to men, from the chaos of creationism to the grand order of evolution, and from watering hole to civilization. Yet, we are worse than the apes that walked upright when we fail to seek the higher things, when we fail to do some good this day.

Said Paul: "Whatsoever things are true, whatsoever things are honest, whatsoever things are just, whatsoever things are pure, whatsoever things are lovely, whatsoever things are of good report; if there be any virtue, and if there be any praise, think on these things" (Philippians 4:8).

THE GREAT PYRAMID HOAX

Bertrand Russell:

I also like the men who study the Great Pyramid, with a view to deciphering its mystical lore. Many great books have been written on this subject, some of which have been presented to me by their authors. It is a singular fact that the Great Pyramid always predicts the history of the world accurately up to the date of publication of the book in question, but after that date it becomes less reliable. Generally the author expects, very soon, wars in Egypt, followed by Armageddon and the coming of Antichrist, but by this time so many people have been recognized as Antichrist that the reader is reluctantly driven to skepticism.

he subject of Egypt and the pyramids often induces a sort of drunkenness of the intellect in many people. Their reasoning powers are put on hold; their very eyesight is blurred, as when it is claimed that the great stones were moved by telepathic means—this when murals show the stones being dragged on huge sleds pulled by over a hundred men as the taskmaster beats out the rhythm of the work.

"PARADISE OF EXILES"

Expelled from Oxford at the age of nineteen for having published anonymously *The Necessity of Atheism*,[1] the poet Shelley spent "his brief impetuous life" in "great controversy and, like Byron, he lives on outside his verse."

Said the poet Kathleen Raine, "In his art if not in his life, Shelley was able to soar, to give expression to those dreams and visions which, continually broken by reality, are inextinguishable in the human heart."

Shelley spent his last years in Italy, his "paradise of exiles," where he was drowned at age thirty in a boating accident on his return from a visit with the poet Byron at Pisa. And true to poetry, when his body washed ashore, it was not buried, but burned on a pyre.

But let us speak not of death, but of life. So now to visit some young poets on a summer's day in 1820. As we approach, we hear the laughter of a party. Keats is 25, Shelley is 28, and Byron is 32.

---

1. Shelley also wrote "Queen Mab" (1813), another anti-religious statement and privately printed poem.

Of Oxford, Matthew Arnold said: "Beautiful city! so venerable, so lovely, so unravaged by the fierce intellectual life of our century, so serene!...whispering from her towers the last enchantments of the Middle Age...Home of lost causes, and forsaken beliefs, and unpopular names, and impossible loyalties!"

THE QUINTESSENTIAL CRIME

Percy Bysshe Shelley (1792–1822):

"The crime of inquiry is one which religion never has for-given."

"THE GOSPEL OF SALVATION BY COMMON SENSE"

In a "peaceful garden," the Greek Epicurus (c. 342–270 B.C.E.) "preached the gospel of salvation by common sense," and as editor R. E. Latham adds, "it impinged with all the force of divine revelation on the sensitive soul of one Roman Citizen, by the name Titus Lucretius Carus, who happened also to be one of the world's supremely great poets.

"The Epicurean gospel was spread by zealous missionaries throughout the Greek world, and a century or so after the Master's death it was preached within the walls of all-conquering Rome (175 B.C.E.)." Epicurus, who adopted the theory of atoms taught by Democritus, had taught that the pursuit of pleasure regulated by prudence, honor, and justice was the goal of man.

"Not the least," writes translator Ronald E. Latham, "Lucretius was addressing us. There is no other ancient writer who speaks more directly to the modern reader."

The influence of the Hebrews on Western thought cannot be minimized, but our scientific and political world was born in pagan Greece. From there came the first light of reason and first breath of freedom.

"A LIFE WORTHY OF THE GODS"

Lucretius (c. 96–55 B.C.E.):

> So it is with men. Though education may apply a sim-
> ilar polish to various individuals, it still leaves funda-
> mental traces of their several temperaments. . . . I
> cannot even find names for the multiplicity of atom-
> ic shapes that give rise to this variety of types. But I
> am clear that there is one relevant fact I can affirm:
> the lingering traces of inborn temperament that can-
> not be eliminated by philosophy are so slight that
> there is nothing to prevent men from leading a life
> worthy of the gods."

Thus, Santayana called the pursuit of "nobility and
excellence" the highest religion. And as Cicero said, "No
praise, then, is too great for philosophy!"

"WHEN HUMAN LIFE LAY GROVELLING"

Lucretius:

> When human life lay grovelling in all men's sight, crushed to the earth under the dead weight of superstition whose grim features loured menacingly upon mortals from the four quarters of the sky, a man of Greece was first to raise mortal eyes in defiance, first to stand erect and brave the challenge. Fables of the gods did not crush him, nor the lightning flash and growling menace of the sky. Rather, they quickened his manhood, so that he, first of all men, longed to smash the constraining locks of nature's doors. The vital vigor of his mind prevailed. He ventured far out beyond the flaming ramparts of the world and voyaged in mind throughout infinity. Returning victorious, he proclaimed to us what can be and what cannot: how a limit is fixed to the power of everything and an immovable frontier post.[1] Therefore superstition in its turn lies crushed beneath his feet, and we by his triumph are lifted level with the skies.

This praise for Epicurus might well be our own praise for the Greeks, for they were the people who first broke the chains of the mind.

---

1. In other words, the myths cannot be true; we must rely on science for our explanations of the real world.

For stealing fire as a gift for man,
Zeus had Prometheus chained to a rock, suffering each
day as an eagle came to eat his liver, which grew back at
night. Illustration: "Prometheus and the Ocean Nymphs,"
by German artist Eduard Müller (1828–1895).

"BEYOND THE RAMPARTS OF THE WORLD"

Lucretius:

Take first the pure and undimmed lustre of the sky and all that it enshrines; the stars that roam across its surface, the moon and the surpassing splendour of the sunlight. If all these sights were now displayed to mortal view for the first time by a swift, unforeseen revelation, what miracle could be recounted greater than this? What would men before the revelation have been less prone to conceive as possible? Nothing, surely. So marvellous would have been that sight—a sight which no one now, you will admit, thinks worthy of an upward glance into the luminous regions of the sky. So has satiety blunted the appetite of our eyes. Desist, therefore, from thrusting out reason from your mind because of its disconcerting novelty. Weigh it, rather, with discerning judgement. Then, if it seems to you true, give in. If it is false, gird yourself to oppose it. For the mind wants to discover by reasoning what exists in the infinity of space that lies out there, beyond the ramparts of the world— that region into which the intellect longs to peer and into which the free projection of the mind does actually extend its flight.[1]

---

1. It is "in the highest degree unlikely that this earth and sky are the only ones to have been created." "Material objects are of two kinds, atoms and compounds of atoms." A voice from two thousand years ago!

"Thought"

by Henri Chapu (1833–1891), a French sculptor. A statue
for the tomb of Comtesse d'Agoult. Note the books by the
great humanists—Marcus Aurelius, Spinoza, and Goethe.

IN DEFENSE OF DOCTRINE

Christian Morgenstern (1805–1867):

> "For, he argues razor-witted,
> That can't be which is not permitted."

Morgenstern, a German lyric poet, was probably not thinking of religious doctrine when he wrote "The Impossible Fact" about obedience to traffic laws. The lines are reminiscent of Thomas Huxley's remark about one theory on the origin of human fingerprints. "A beautiful theory, killed by a nasty, ugly little fact."

**A preacher pointing to Scripture,
arguing with an angel from God!**

"UNBORN HISTORICAL INCIDENTS"

Mark Twain (Samuel Clemens, 1835–1910):

> Along through the book I have distributed a few anachronisms and unborn historical incidents and such things, so as to help the tale over the difficult places. The idea is not original with me; I got it out of Herodotus. Herodotus says, "Very few things happen at the right time, and the rest do not happen at all: the conscientious historian will correct these defects."[1]

On "Fire and Brimstone"

> This nightmare occupied some ten pages of manuscript and wound up with a sermon so destructive of all hope to non-Presbyterians that it took first prize.
>
> *   *   *
>
> [I]t was an argument that dealt in limitless fire and brimstone and thinned the predestined elect down to a company so small as to be hardly worth the saving.

Presbyterianism has its origins in the hell-fire predestination philosophy of John Calvin. As the dictator of Geneva, Switzerland, John Calvin had Michael Servetus (1511–1553) burned at the stake for opposing infant baptism and the doctrine of the trinity in the book *De Trinitatis Erroribus*. Servetus was a martyr for religious tolerance and freedom of thought! Pray for us, Saint Michael Servetus!

---

1. Or so Mark Twain said of Herodotus in his preface to *A Horse's Tale*. Herodotus, a Greek historian of the fifth century B.C.E. is known as the "Father of History," but also by his critics as "The Father of Lies."

"PHRASES THAT STRIKE LIKE BULLETS"

Although Emily Dickinson was as "certain of heaven" as if "the chart were given," she grew obsessed in her latter years with death. Perhaps this was a result of her reclusive life; she worked in isolation without the benefit of criticism, and only four of her poems found print in her lifetime. None of her thousand-and-more poems bore a title. But shine, she did, nevertheless!

"At her best," observes Robert N. Linscott, "she writes as Thoreau wished to live—close to the bone, concentrating the very essence of what she saw and felt in phrases that strike and penetrate like bullets, with an originality of thought unsurpassed in American poetry."

In the following one of four stanzas, though the intent may be religious, the philosopher cannot but smile in delight at thoughts of spring.

> The skies can't keep their secret!
> They tell it to the hills—
> The hills just tell the orchards—
> And they the daffodils!

"THERE IS NO FRIGATE LIKE A BOOK"

Emily Dickinson (1830–1886):

> There is no frigate like a book
>   To take us lands away,
> Nor any coursers[1] like a page
>   Of prancing poetry.
>
> This traverse may the poorest take
>   Without oppress of toll;
> How frugal is the chariot
>   That bears a human soul!

---

1. courser: a swift horse, as in Shelley's "Prometheus Unbound," where a spirit says,

> "My coursers are fed with the lightning,
> They drink of the whirlwind's stream,
> And when the red morning is bright'ning
> They bathe in the fresh sunbeam."

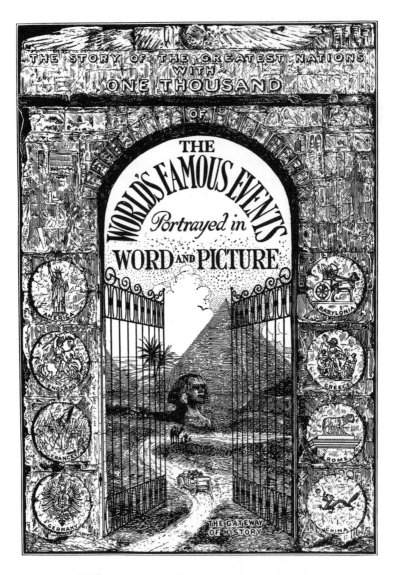

"There is no frigate like a book."

How delightful is this illustration from the frontispiece of
The World Famous Events, a nine-volume world history
from 1913. And off we go through the "Gateway of History"—our frigate an old roadster!

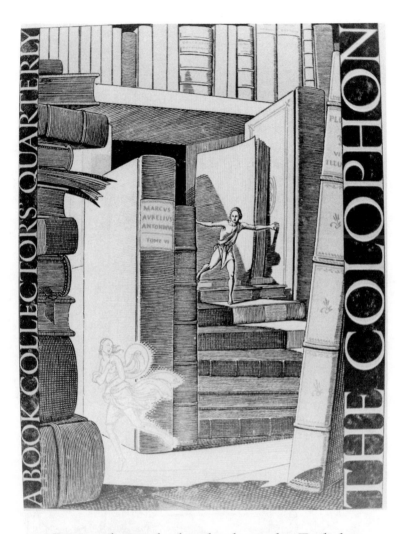

Down the path that leads to the Eighth Continent,
the Republic of Letters, the Land of Books

THE CONQUEST OF FEAR

Bertrand Russell:

Fear sometimes operates directly, by inventing rumors of disaster in wartime, or by imaging objects of terror, such as ghosts, sometimes it operates indirectly, by creating belief in something comforting, such as the elixir of life, or heaven for ourselves and hell for our enemies. Fear has many forms—fear of death, fear of the dark, fear of the unknown, fear of the herd, and that vague generalized fear that comes to those who conceal from themselves their more specific terrors. Until you have admitted your own fears to yourself, and have guarded yourself by a difficult effort of will against their myth-making power, you cannot hope to think truly about many matters of great importance, especially those with which religious beliefs are concerned. Fear is the main source of superstition and one of the main sources of cruelty. To conquer fear is the beginning of wisdom, in the pursuit of truth as in the endeavor after a worthy manner of life.

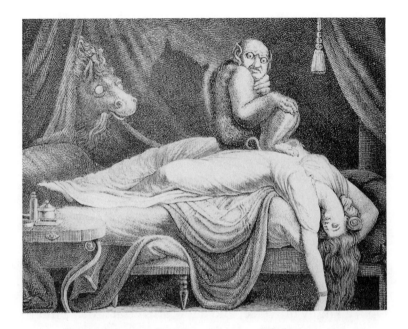

Philosophy refutes our nightmares

and brings our mind back to itself and daylight. If we are of a mystical temperament, it bathes our religion in liberality and refinement. The god and devils of punishment are left far behind. And to the doubter, it says fear not and live this day. And of fear, we can also profit from a story by St. Augustine. A philosopher was aboard a ship captained by a bad man, and after a violent storm, the fearless captain jeered the philosopher for his terror. Said the philosopher, quoting from a similar incident that occurred to the pagan Aristippus, "A rogue need not worry about losing his worthless life, but Aristippus has a duty to care for a life like his."

"The Nightmare," by Henry Fuseli (1741–1825)

"HE CAME TO PREACH HIS GOSPEL"

Said editor Carl Bode: "In his *Ralph Waldo Emerson,* issued in 1885, the sprightly and ordinarily irreverent Oliver Wendell Holmes couched his praise in the highest of religious terms. What was the mission of which Emerson visited our earth? Holmes asked. The answer was that he came to preach his gospel to us."

Emerson "rejected Judaism as austere, Buddhism as esoteric, Christianity as fossilized. Gradually he clarified what he did want. The essentials were simple: a kindly God, a kindly universe, and a few universal laws." And to account for evil? "There is a crack in every thing God has made."

> But men are better than their theology. Their daily life gives it the lie. Every ingenuous and aspiring soul leaves the doctrine behind him in his own experience, and all men feel sometimes the falsehood which they cannot demonstrate. For men are wiser than they know. That which they hear in schools and pulpits without afterthought, if said in conversation would probably be questioned in silence. If a man dogmatize in mixed company on Providence and the divine laws, he is answered by a silence which conveys well enough to an observer the dissatisfaction of the hearer, but his incapacity to make his own statement.

"INTELLECT ANNULS FATE"

Ralph Waldo Emerson (1803–1882):

Intellect annuls Fate. So far as a man thinks, he is free...."Look not on Nature, for her name is fatal," said the oracle. The too much contemplation of these limits induces meanness. They who talk much of destiny, their birth-star, etc., are in a lower dangerous plane, and invite the evils they fear.

And as for those bound to zodiacs, bibles, and ancient times:

"What have I to do," asks the impatient reader, "with jasper and sardonyx, beryl and chalcedony; what with arks and passovers, ephahs and ephods; what with lepers and emerods; what with heave-offerings and unleavened bread; chariots of fire, dragons crowned and horned, behemoth and unicorn? Good for orientals,[1] these are nothing to me. The more learning you bring to explain them, the more glaring the impertinence. The more coherent and elaborate the system, the less I like it. I say, with the Spartan, 'Why do you speak so much to the purpose, of that which is nothing to the purpose?' My learning is such as God gave me in my birth and habit, in the delight and study of my eyes, and not of another man's."

---

1. Best thought of as a reference to freedom of thought versus submission to authority

VINTAGE WINE
(FROM THE ESSAY, "SELF RELIANCE")

Ralph Waldo Emerson:

"For every Stoic was a Stoic; but in Christendom where is the Christian?"

* * *

"A foolish consistency is the hobgoblin of little minds, adored by little statesmen and philosophers and divines."

* * *

"Honor is venerable to us because it is no ephemera. It is always ancient virtue. We worship it to-day because it is not of today."

* * *

"Society everywhere is in conspiracy against the manhood of every one of its members…. Whoso would be a man, must be a nonconformist."

* * *

A man "now and then wakes up, exercises his reason and finds himself a true prince."

* * *

"If therefore a man claims to know and speak of God and carries you backward to the phraseology of some old mouldered nation in another country, in another world, believe him not…. The centuries are conspirators against the sanity and authority of the soul."

"LIKE A YOUNG GOD"

And Emerson said, "Life is an ecstasy. We know what madness belongs to love,—what power to paint a vile object in hues of heaven."

The people who knew Emerson, said Santayana, "became aware, if we may say so, of the ultraviolet rays of his spectrum, of the inaudible highest notes of his gamut,[1] too pure and thin for common ears."

"He was like a young god making experiments in creation: he blotched the work, and always began again on a new and better plan. Every day he said, 'Let there be light,' and every day the light was new. His sun, like that of Heraclitus, was different every morning.

"No wonder that he brought thence to the tightly conventional minds of his contemporaries a breath as if from paradise."

---

1. gamut: any complete musical scale.

PAGAN VERSUS BIBLICAL MIRACLES
ROMULUS VERSUS SAMSON

Plutarch
(c. 46–120 B.C.E., Romulus, c. 753–716 B.C.E.):

"But what some write [of the battle near Fidenae], that of fourteen thousand that fell that day, above half were slain by Romulus' own hand, verges too near to fable, and is, indeed, simply incredible."

The Bible (Judges 15:15, c. ninth century B.C.E.):

"And he [Samson] found a new jawbone of an ass, and put forth his hand and took it, and slew a thousand men therewith."

"It was for the sake of others," said Plutarch in his *Lives of Noble Greeks*, "that I first commenced writing biographies; but I find myself proceeding and attaching myself to it for my own; the virtues of these great men serving me as a sort of looking-glass, in which I may see how to adjust and adorn my own life."

The pagan Plutarch was a religious man with a "deeply humanist temper." In his essay "On God's Slowness to Punish," he used many arguments, including the notion "that God may be using bad men as tools for producing good." Needless to say, Plutarch's was not the last essay on this impossible subject.

"Samson Smiting the Philistines with the Jawbone of an Ass"

an engraving after Maarten van Heemskerck (1498–1574), a Dutch painter of religious subjects, from a series of engravings depicting "The disasters of the Jewish people as Moral Examples." In the background, Samson is shown pulling down the pillars of a temple.

PAGAN VERSUS BIBLICAL MIRACLES
THE SUN AND A RAIN OF STONES

Livy (59 B.C.E.–17 C.E.), *The War With Hannibal*:

> In the course of that winter [218-217 B.C.E.] many queer things happened in Rome and the country round it—or at least they were said to have happened, and believed...as is the way when men's minds are shaken by superstitious fears. A six-month-old baby, of good family, had shouted "Victory!" in the vegetable market...shapes like shining ships had appeared in the sky...in Picenum it had rained stones; at Caere the divination tablets had ominously grown smaller, and in Gaul a wolf had pulled a sentry's sword out of its sheath and run off with it....
>
> [At Alba (206 B.C.E.)] two suns were said to have been seen...in the country near Rome an ox talked and the altar of Neptune in the Circus Flaminius poured with sweat.... The consuls received instructions by senatorial decree to make atonement for these prodigies by sacrifice of full-grown victims and to hold a day of prayer, and the instructions were duly carried out.

The Bible
(Joshua 10:11–13, c. fifteenth century B.C.E.):

> And it came to pass... that the Lord cast down great stones from heaven upon them... [and more] died with hailstones than they whom the children of Israel slew with the sword....
>
> And the sun stood still, and the moon stayed.... So the sun stood still in the midst of heaven, and hasted not to go down about a whole day.

AND THE WALLS CAME TUMBLING DOWN

Xenophon (c. 434–355 B.C.E., *The Persian Expedition*):

> There was a large deserted city there called Larissa [Nimrud]....At the time when the Persians seized the empire from the Medes, the King...was quite unable to take it. A cloud, however, covered up the sun and hid it from sight until the inhabitants deserted the place, and so the city was taken.
>
> From here a day's march of eighteen miles brought them [the Greeks] to a large undefended fortification near a city called Mespila, which was once inhabited by the Medes... and the King of the Persians, when he besieged the city, could not take it.... Zeus, however, drove the inhabitants out of their wits with a thunderstorm, and so the city was taken.

The Bible
(Joshua 6:2–5 and 10:13, c. fifteenth century B.C.E.):

> And the Lord said unto Joshua, See, I have given into thine hand Jericho.... And seven priests shall bear before the ark seven trumpets of ram's horns: and the seventh day ye shall compass the city seven times.... and when ye hear the sound of the trumpet, all the people shall shout with a great shout: and the wall of the city shall fall down flat....
>
> And the sun stood still, and the moon stayed... and hasted not to go down about a whole day.

PAGAN VERSUS BIBLICAL MIRACLES
THE LOWERING OF THE WATERS

Xenophon:

After this he [the Persian Cyrus] crossed the [Euphrates] river and the whole of the rest of the army followed him. In the crossing no one got wet from the river water above the nipples. The people of Thapsacus said that this river had never except on this occasion been passable on foot, but could only be crossed in boats; and on this occasion Abrocomas had gone ahead and burned the boats to prevent Cyrus from crossing. It seemed certainly that there was something supernatural about it, and that the river had undoubtedly made way for Cyrus since he was destined to become King.[1]

---

1. Xenophon joined the expedition of Cyrus the Younger against Cyrus's brother Artaxerxes II of Persia (Iran), and after Cyrus was killed at the battle of Cunaxa (401 B.C.E.), Xenophon guided the Greek mercenaries out of hostile Persia. Stumbling up one last hill after a thousand-mile march, the Greeks cried, "The Sea! The Sea!"

Of *The Persian Expedition* (the so-called *Anabasis*), editor George Calkwell said: "Let barbarians fall to the ground in submission to whoever wins the contest for the crown. The Greeks will give their allegiance to the man whose reason, not his blood, proves his fitness to lead." Such was the message of Xenophon. At the same time, it must be remembered that "Persia was one of the chief civilizing forces of history, and the Greeks in calling them 'barbarians,' as they called all who did not speak Greek, have greatly misled posterity."

Before the war, Xenophon was a devoted student of Socrates.

THE PARTING OF THE WATERS?

The Bible (Exodus 14:21–30):

And Moses stretched out his hand over the sea; and the LORD caused the sea to go back by a strong wind all that night,[1] and made the sea dry land, and the waters were divided. And the children of Israel went into the midst of the sea upon dry ground: and the waters were a wall unto them on the their right hand and on their left.

And the Egyptians pursued.... And the waters returned, and covered the chariots, and the horsemen, and all the host of Pharaoh that came into the sea after them.... Thus the LORD saved Israel that day out of the hand of the Egyptians.

---

1. This story sounds less like a miracle and more like a natural phenomenon. Other escaping slaves were probably apprehended when the shallow tidal waters of some coastal region were not blown a good distance off the natural shoreline, allowing passage to the other side of a bay. After all, the sea did not just open, but it took all night to move the waters.

But this would never do for Hollywood. For Cecil B. DeMille, it had to be a real parting of the deep sea.

A COINCIDENCE MOST ODD
MOSES IN THE BULRUSHES

The Bible (Exodus 2:1–5, about 1230 B.C.E.):

> And there went a man of the house of Levi, and took to wife a daughter of Levi. And the woman conceived and bare a son: and when she saw him that he was a goodly child, she hid him three months. And when she could not longer hide him, she took for him an ark of bulrushes, and daubed it with slime and with pitch, and put the child therein, and she laid it in the flags by the river's brink....
>
> And the daughter of the Pharaoh came down to wash herself at the river; and her maidens walked along by the river's side; and when she saw the ark among the flags, she sent her maid to fetch it.

SARGON IN THE BULRUSHES

Cuneiform Babylonian text about Sargon I (c. 2750 B.C.E.):

Sargon, the mighty king, the king of Agade, am I.
My mother was a priestess, my father I knew not,
And the brother of my father dwells in the mountain.
My city is Azupiranu, which lies on the bank of the Euphrates.
My vestal [chaste, pure] mother conceived me, in secret she brought me forth.
She set me in a basket of rushes, with bitumen[1] she closed my door;
She cast me into the river, which rose not over me.
The river bore me up, unto Akki, the irrigator, it carried me.
Akki, the irrigator... lifted me out,
Akki, the irrigator, as his own son... reared me,
Akki... as his gardener appointed me.
While I was a gardener the goddess Ishtar loved me,
And for... four years I ruled the kingdom.

---

1. bitumen: pitch, but also tar.

According to legend,

Sargon's mother made "a basket of rushes" and set him adrift on the Euphrates River, and the baby was found and brought up by a gardener. Then one day a beautiful woman appeared to the young Sargon out of a cloud of doves. Not knowing that she was the goddess Ishtar (Astarte, for whom doves were sacred), Sargon nevertheless treated her in princely fashion, and she fell in love with him. Later under Ishtar's guidance, Sargon rose to unite all the land of Babylonia under one rule.

A legend modified and borrowed to glorify Moses?

"The Goddess Ishtar," by American artist Edwin J. Prittie

"Moses in the Bullrushes"

When the daughter of the Pharaoh "saw the ark among the flags, she sent her maid to fetch it" (Exodus 1:5). Moses was then raised by his own mother, who was called to tend the lost infant.

Painting by Paul Delaroche (1797–1856), a French artist

TO CURE BLINDNESS WITH SPIT

Were both John and Suetonius repeating stories derived from the folk medicine of the ancient Near East, which claimed that saliva can somehow cure blindness? The parallel incidents were mentioned by David Hume in his essay "Of Miracles."

The pagan miracle occurred in Egypt when the Roman Emperor Vespasian (69–70 C.E.) was in Alexandria, and interestingly, Serapis, an Egyptian god of the underworld, appeared on Roman coins with Isis on the reverse during Vespasian's reign. Isis, the chief female deity of the Egyptians, was a mother-goddess often depicted as suckling the child Harpokrates (Horus). The early excessive veneration of the Virgin and Christ Child probably owed something to the cult of Isis that had spread from Egypt throughout the Roman Empire.

The Gospel of John was not written until c. 78–90 C.E. in Ephesus, capital of the Roman province of Asia, now on the coast of Turkey. It would seem reasonable that many incidents were attributed to Jesus not out of actual fact, but out of love of Jesus and of Christianity, the desire to impress nonbelievers and gain converts, and finally, out of the natural desire to believe that miracles really do occur.

A BLIND COINCIDENCE

Suetonius (c. 69–140 C.E.):

As he [Vespasian] sat on the Tribunal, two laborers, one blind, the other lame, approached together, begging to be healed. Apparently the god Serapis had promised them in a dream that if Vespasian would consent to spit in the blind man's eyes, and touch the lame man's leg with his heel, both would be made well. Vespasian had so little faith in his curative powers that he showed a great reluctance . . . but his friends persuaded him to try them, in the presence of a large audience, too—and the charm worked.

The Bible (John 9:1–7; c. 78–90 C.E.)

And as Jesus passed by, he saw a man which was blind from his birth… [and] he spat on the ground and made clay of the spittle, and he anointed the eyes of the blind man with clay. And said unto him, Go wash in the pool of Siloam. . . . He went his way therefore, and washed, and came seeing.

IT GIVES US PAUSE

Embedded in the worldly wisdom of Lucretius is the pagan language that would be adopted by Christianity. And how strange the phrases seem when removed from familiar context! We have grown so used to the poetry of praise for the Virgin Mary that we are oddly moved to hear this same poetry as an echo out of the past, an echo of praises for a revered pagan goddess!

The goddess Venus on a Lion[1]

---

1. See page 83 of present volume.

PAGAN ECHOES IN CHRISTIANITY

Lucretius:

This is she [the mother of the gods] who was hymned by Grecian poets adept in ancient lore. They pictured her a goddess, driving a chariot drawn by a yoke of lions. By this they signified that the whole mighty mass hangs in airy space: for earth cannot rest on earth. They harnessed wild beasts, because the fiercest of children cannot but be softened and subdued by the duty owned to parents. Upon her head they set a battlemented crown, because earth in selected spots is fortified and bears the weight of cities. Decked with this emblem even now the image of the Holy Mother is borne about the world in solemn state. Various nations hail her with time-honoured ceremony as our Lady of Ida.

* * *

Bear this well in mind, and you will immediately perceive that nature is free and uncontrolled by proud masters and runs the universe by herself without the aid of the gods. For who—by the sacred hearts of the gods who pass their unruffled lives, their placid aeon, in calm and peace!—who can rule the sum total of the measureless?

"OUR ORACLES, OUR TRIPODS"

Voltaire:

"Let us trust to ourselves, see all with our own eyes;
Let these be our oracles, our tripods and our gods."

"Oracles" and "tripods" refer to the ancient Oracle at Delphi, who sat over a chasm on a three-legged chair to pronounce her prophecies. In the years before Athens became a republic, she was ruled by the tyrant Hippias, and the Oracle at Delphi told the Spartans that they must help overthrow Hippias. The priesthood at Delphi was richly rewarded by the Athenians for encouraging the Spartans.

"The Oracle Of Delphi"

by Henri Motte (1846–1922), a French painter. Note the stairway and snakes below the tripod chair over a chasm.

A FOUNTAIN OF HERESY

Voltaire was a fountain of heresy, and one of his little-known but fine works is *The Questions of Zapata*, which purports to be sixty-six questions by the licentiate Zapata,[1] who, "being appointed Professor of Theology at the University of Salamanca, presented these questions to a committee of doctors in 1629."

Set in the dark days of Spain, the outcome of Zapata's questions is foreordained.

"The Birth of Venus"

---

1. Licentiate: In Europe, a degree between baccalaureate and doctorate. Also, one who has a licence to practice a particular profession.

"The Birth of Venus" by nineteenth-century French sculptor Louis Pierre Gustave Fort.

THE CRIMES OF ZAPATA

Voltaire:

The Questions of Zapata

Question 10:

What shall I say of the garden of Eden, from which issued a river which divided into four rivers—the Tigris, Euphrates, Phison (which is believed to be the Phasis), and Gihon, which flows in Ethiopia, and must therefore be the Nile, the source of which is a thousand miles from the source of the Euphrates? I shall be told once more that God is a very poor geographer.

Question 12:

How shall I explain the story of angels who fell in love with the daughters of men, and begot giants?[1] May I not be told that this episode is borrowed from pagan legends?

---

1. "There were giants in the earth in those days; and...the sons of God came in unto the daughters of men, and they bare children to them" (Genesis 6:4). See Genesis 2:10-14 for the rivers of Eden.

PRAY GOD FOR BROTHER ZAPATA

Voltaire:

[The Last Question of Zapata]

Wise Masters,

...tell me what I must do with those who doubt? Must I, for their edification, have the ordinary and extraordinary question[1] put to them?

I await the honor of your reply.

> Dominico Zapata
> y verdadero, y honrado,
> y caricativo.

Zapata, receiving no answer, took to preaching God in all simplicity. He announced to men the common father, the rewarder, punisher, and pardoner. He extricated the truth from the lies, and separated religion from fanaticism; he taught and practiced virtue. He was gentle, kindly, and modest; and he was burned at Valladolid in the year of grace 1631. Pray God for the soul of Brother Zapata.

---

1. How darkly humorous this "extraordinary question." The tortures of the "Holy Office," or Inquisition. Sometimes it is said that the Church used the very persuasive "argument" of the rack against heretics.

Note that Valladolid (above) was the hometown of Tomas de Torquemada (1420–1498), the "inquisitor general" of Spain. During his fifteen years of atrocity, two thousand human beings were burned alive at the stake and thousands of others tortured for heresy.

"Tribunal of the Inquisition"

At the signal of "the black-robed clerk of the Holy Office....The victim is drawn towards the ceiling, his feet pulled down by cruel weights. Pale and feeble, shuddering, a broken wretch, his soul gives way to fright, and he cries at length, 'Pity!' Then the Chief Inquisitor, who has begun the trial in tones of mild persuasion, suddenly glares cat-like, stretches out his skinny finger, and seizes the last moment of his victim's consciousness to cry, 'will you confess now?'"

Illustration by Aldophe Steinheil (1850–1908), a French painter

"The Creation of Eve"

in a woodcut by Albrecht Dürer (1471–1528), a master engraver and leader of the German Renaissance school of painting.

Yet, did this really happen, or is it a religious myth?

A Comparison of science with the Adam and Eve myth

Detail from the "Tower of Time," by John Gurche. At the top is a Neanderthal man, his face aglow in firelight. In the larger painting, faces of three modern humans rise above the head of the Neanderthal man.

THE RAFT OF CREDULITY

Voltaire:

The Questions of Zapata

Question 13:

How shall I get out of the deluge, the cataracts of heaven (which has no cataracts), and the animals coming from Japan, Africa, America, and the south, and being enclosed in a large ark with food and drink for one year, without counting the time when the earth was still too damp to produce food for them? How did Noah's little family manage to give all these animals their proper food?[1] It consisted only of eight persons.

---

1. Consider a modern zoo, even the largest of which only has a fraction of the species of animals on earth. Consider the tons of food needed each and every day to feed the animals in the San Diego Zoo. And consider what the meat eaters on the Ark eat? On second thought, don't consider these things. They muddy up a nice story.

As the ark drifts away

the mass of humanity drowns—innocent men, women, and children crying in vain for salvation. Interpreted literally, the Flood story becomes an argument for atheism. Yet, did all of humanity except a single family really die in a flood?

"The Deluge," by Melchior Lorck

Religion

"Adam and Eve Seduced by the Demon." Was there ever really a tree with magical fruit that gave knowledge to those who partook of it? And a talking serpent? Deep down inside we know the answers to these questions. The Paradise or Garden of Eden story is a dream, a Shangri-la with a moral lesson. We know it well: Beyond the mountains of the Blue Moon is a place of enchantment where no one ever grows old. "Tell it again, Father. And don't leave out the part about the angel with a flaming sword."

"Let's see, once upon a time . . . ."

"Adam and Eve Seduced by the Demon," by an anonymous Italian artist of the sixteenth century

"The Professor and His Pupil" [1]

From the moment men began to study, to question the basis of authority, and to ask serious questions about their cherished beliefs, the story of Adam and Eve was doomed as an explanation for the origin of man.

Some things never change, though. The student seems more interested in the dogs than in the professor, who is lost in a search for something on a giant globe. What are the titles of the volumes on these shelves? we wonder. Note the details.

---

1. Engraving from a painting by John Bagnold Burgess

"FILL ME WITH A BUOYANT DOUBT"

Louis Untermeyer (1885–1977):

> Ever insurgent let me be,
>> Make me more daring than devout:
> From sleek contentment keep me free,
>> And fill me with a buoyant doubt.

In his "Prayer," Untermeyer also asks God to, "Give me the Heart to fight—and lose." And in the final stanza:

> From compromise and things half-done,
>> Keep me, with stern and stubborn pride.
> And when, at last, the fight is won,
>> God, keep me still unsatisfied.

Great men and women pray great things, their religious perspectives crossing all horizons. Mr. Untermeyer was an American author and gifted poetry editor.

"THE CHASTITY OF THE INTELLECT"

George Santayana:

Scepticism is the chastity of the intellect, and it is shameful to surrender it too soon or to the first comer: there is nobility in preserving it coolly and proudly through a long youth, until at last, in the ripeness of instinct and discretion, it can be safely exchanged for fidelity and happiness.[1]

---

1. Santayana, *Scepticism and Animal Faith* (1923). The "animal" refers to the "workaday opinions" and assumptions of humankind.

"THE ARABIAN NIGHTS"

Sir Richard Burton's life speaks to the heart of every arm-chair adventurer, and he is forever that quintessential explorer standing on some hill of a lost continent and before him, "A rose-red city 'half as old as Time!'" [1]

Burton's life was romance. Though not born in the Renaissance, he was a true Renaissance man, a master of dozens of languages, translator of the sixteen-volume *Arabian Nights* (1885–1888), an adventurer and ethnologist who made a pilgrimage to Mecca disguised as an Arab, a great explorer who attempted to find the source of the Nile, a scholar, master swordsman, and "superb raconteur."

It seems appropriate that in literature Richard Burton awoke from death on the banks of Philip Jose Farmer's "River World," and there with Mark Twain, Alice in Wonderland, and even Joan of Arc, he continued his life of adventure on a ten-million-mile river.

---

1. John William Burgon (1813–1860), "Petra," the Newdigate Prize Poem. Part of the line comes from Samuel Rogers (1763–1855), "Italy, A Farewell": "By many a temple half as old as Time!"

"AFRESH DAWNS THE MORN OF LIFE"

Richard Burton (1821–1890):

> Of the gladdest moments in human life, methinks, is the departure upon a distant journey into unknown lands. Shaking off with one mighty effort the fetters of Habit, the leaden weight of Routine, the cloak of many Cares and the slavery of Home, man feels once more happy. The blood flows with the fast circulation of childhood. . . . Afresh dawns the morn of life.

"Aurora," goddess of dawn, by Giovanni Francesco Barbieri (1592–1662)

The spirit of adventure knows no age.

"An adventurous child, thanks to the gods," said the Latin poet Horace (65–8 B.C.E.). Here we see Frank Fairweather, who "danced down the road" as he left home for an "adventure on Land and Sea." From *Frank Fairweather's Fortunes* (1895).

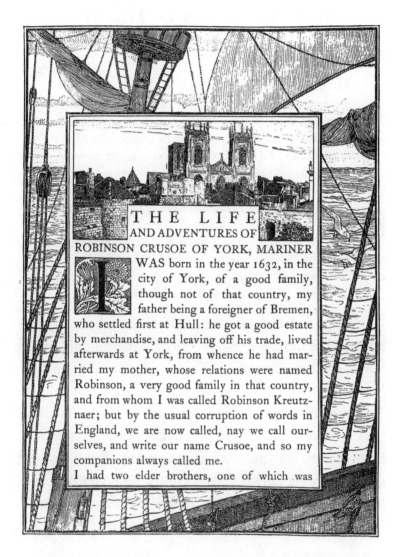

THE LIFE
AND ADVENTURES OF
ROBINSON CRUSOE OF YORK, MARINER

I WAS born in the year 1632, in the city of York, of a good family, though not of that country, my father being a foreigner of Bremen, who settled first at Hull: he got a good estate by merchandise, and leaving off his trade, lived afterwards at York, from whence he had married my mother, whose relations were named Robinson, a very good family in that country, and from whom I was called Robinson Kreutznaer; but by the usual corruption of words in England, we are now called, nay we call ourselves, and write our name Crusoe, and so my companions always called me.

I had two elder brothers, one of which was

What a debt we owe you, Mr. Daniel Defoe!

No explanation is necessary as we begin to read page one of a 1900 edition of your book.

JEFFERSON'S JESUS

Thomas Jefferson (1743–1826):

> Abstracting what is really his [Jesus'] from the rubbish
> in which it is buried, easily distinguished by its lustre
> from the dross of His biographers, and as separable
> from that as the diamond from the dunghill, we have
> the outlines of a system of the most sublime morality
> which has ever fallen from the lips of man; outlines of
> which it is lamentable He did not live to fill up. . . .
> The establishment of the innocent and genuine char-
> acter of this benevolent Moralist, and the rescuing it
> from the imputation of imposture, which has resulted
> from artificial systems, invented by the ultra-
> Christian sects, unauthorized by a single word ever
> uttered by Him, is a most desirable object.[1]

Although Jefferson believed in God and the immortality of the human spirit, he rejected traditional Christianity. For him, Jesus was "a man of illegitimate birth."[2]
Jefferson was specific in the doctrines he did not believe:
"The immaculate conception of Jesus, His deification,
the creation of the world by Him, His miraculous powers,
His resurrection and visible Ascension, His corporeal
presence in the Eucharist, the Trinity, original sin, atone-
ment, regeneration, election, orders of Hierarchy, etc."[3]

---

1. Jefferson's letter to William Short, written at Monticello, October 31, 1819.

2. Letter of August 10, 1787, to Peter Carr, Jefferson's nephew.

3. Letter to William Short, October 31, 1819.

THIS ALSO IS PHILOSOPHY

Jesus of Nazareth (John 8:1–9):

> Jesus went unto the mount of Olives. And early in the morning he came again to the temple, and all the people came unto him; and he sat down, and taught them. And the scribes and Pharisees brought unto him a woman taken in adultery: and when they had set her in the midst, They say unto him, Master this woman was taken in adultery, in the very act. Now Moses in the law commanded us that such should be stoned: but what sayest thou?
>
> This they said, tempting him, that they might have to accuse him. But Jesus stooped down, and with his finger wrote on the ground, as though he heard them not.
>
> So when they continued asking him, he lifted up himself, and said unto them, He that is without sin among you, let him first cast a stone at her. And again he stooped down, and wrote on the ground. And they, which heard it, being convicted by their own conscience, went out one by one, beginning at the eldest, even unto the last: and Jesus was left alone and the woman standing in the midst.

Thus, we read philosophy, and as Jesus said—for who could say it better?—"Judge not, that ye be not judged" (Matthew 7:1).

THE TRUE BELIEVER

In 1951, Eric Hoffer published his *True Believer*, "a brilliant and frightening study of the mind of the fanatic." Hoffer, a longshoreman turned philosopher, analyzed mass movements from Christianity to Communism to find their common elements in a work of devastating insight and "Machiavellian detachment."

> The opposite of the religious fanatic is not the fanatical atheist but the gentle cynic who cares not whether there is a God or not. The atheist is a religious person. He believes in atheism as though it were a new religion. He is an atheist with devoutness and unction. According to Renan, "The day after that on which the world should no longer believe in God, atheists would be the wretchedest of all men."
>
> * * *
>
> They [all fanatics] are as far apart and close together as Saul and Paul. And it is easier for a fanatic Communist to be converted to fascism, chauvinism or Catholicism than to become a sober liberal.

DOCTRINE MUST BE UNINTELLIGIBLE

Eric Hoffer (1902–1983):

If a doctrine is not unintelligible, it has to be vague; and if neither unintelligible nor vague, it has to be unverifiable. One has to get to heaven or the distant future to determine the truth of an effective doctrine. When some part of a doctrine is relatively simple, there is a tendency among the faithful to complicate and obscure it. Simple words are made pregnant with meaning and made to look like symbols in a secret message. There is thus an illiterate air about the most literate true believer. He seems to use words as if he were ignorant of their true meaning. Hence, too, his taste for quibbling, hair-splitting and scholastic tortuousness.

DREAMS
INEXTINGUISHABLE

The poet Kathleen Raine sang these praises, "In his art if not in his life, Shelley was able to soar, to give expression to those dreams and visions which, continually broken by reality, are inextinguishable in the human spirit." In quoting Raine, the modern editor Isabel Quigly spoke of the "idealized but unmistakable" self-portrait of Shelley in his poem "Alastor."

> The brave, the gentle, and the beautiful,
>   The child of grace and genius.

Isabel Quigly added that in his life "Shelley aroused... enormous personal virulence, and even today... he can still raise temperatures and conjure violent antagonisms as a man. . . . Shelley lives on outside his verse, and continues still to attract or repel, as he did when he was alive."

Louis Untermeyer expressed it this way: "Misjudged as a licentious pagan by a self-righteous world, he was essentially a passionate believer in universal goodness, even in human perfectibility."

"GOOD, GREAT AND JOYOUS, BEAUTIFUL AND FREE"

Percy Bysshe Shelley (1792–1822):

> To suffer woes which Hope thinks infinite;
> To forgive wrongs darker than death or night;
>   To defy Power, which seems omnipotent;
> To love, and bear; to hope till Hope creates
> From its own wreck the thing it contemplates;
>   Neither to change, nor falter, nor repent;
> This, like thy glory, Titan, is to be
> Good, great and joyous, beautiful and free;
> This alone Life, Joy, Empire, and Victory.

In Greek mythology, Prometheus stole fire from heaven and taught man its use, and for this crime, Zeus had him chained to a rock. Each day an eagle (or vulture) came to eat his liver, which grew anew each night.

Prometheus was a Titan, a member of the race of giant gods.

"ALL GREAT THINGS COME SLOWLY TO BIRTH"

John Tyndall (1820–1893), for twenty years superinten-
dent of the Royal Institution, contributed much to the
dissemination of knowledge by bringing science to the
reading public. As a physicist and a believer in God, he
held that the book of Genesis "is a poem, not a scientific
treatise," and of Darwin's *Origin of the Species*:

> All great things come slowly to birth. Copernicus, as
> I informed you, pondered his great work for thirty-
> three years. Newton for nearly twenty years kept the
> idea of Gravitation before his mind. . . . Darwin for
> two-and-twenty years pondered the problem of the
> origin of the species, and doubtless he would have
> continued to do so had he not found Wallace upon
> his track.

Alfred Russell Wallace arrived at the idea of evolution by natural selection independently of Darwin, and
the "behavior of Mr. Wallace in relation to this subject
has been dignified in the highest degree." In light of the
passion to claim first discovery of a great idea, the conduct of these two men is a model for all time and the ideal
of philosophy. It is now common to speak of the Darwin-
Wallace theory of evolution.

IN PRAISE OF DARWIN

John Tyndall:

"The Abraham of science—a searcher as obedient to the command of truth as was the patriarch to the command of God."

Said Darwin,

> During these two years I was led to think much about religion. Whilst on board the Beagle I was quite orthodox, and I remember being heartily laughed at by several of the officers (though themselves orthodox) for quoting the Bible as an unanswerable authority on some point of morality. I suppose it was the novelty of the argument that amused them. But I had gradually come by this time (1836–39), to see that the Old Testament was no more to be trusted than the sacred books of the Hindoos. The question then continually rose before my mind and would not be banished,—is it credible that if God were now to make a revelation to the Hindoos, he would permit it to be connected with the belief in Vishnu, Siva, &c., as Christianity is connected with the Old Testament? This appeared to me utterly incredible....
>
> Thus disbelief crept over me at a very slow rate, but was at last complete. The rate was so slow that I felt no distress.

AN AUTHORITY LIKE CLAY

John Tyndall:

> Profoundly interesting, and indeed pathetic,[1] to me
> are those attempts of the opening mind of man to
> appease its hunger for a cause. But the book of
> Genesis has no voice in scientific questions. To the
> grasp of geology, which it resisted for a time, it at
> length yielded like potter's clay; its authority as a sys-
> tem of cosmogony being discredited on all hands, by
> the abandonment of the obvious meaning of its
> writer. It is a poem, not a scientific treatise.

Creation: 9 A.M., October 23, 4004 B.C.E.

The King James Bible was first published in 1611, and
later a chronology, worked out by Bishop James Ussher
(1581–1656), was inserted in its margins. Bishop Ussher
calculated that the creation took place in 4004 B.C.E.
Another man, Dr. John Lightfoot (1602–1675), vice-chan-
cellor of the University of Cambridge, put the creation of
man at 9 A.M. on October 23, 4004 B.C.E.

---

1. pathetic: used in the sense of arousing sympathy, a moving experience.

"The Creation of the Fish and Birds"
by the French artist Paul Gustave Doré (1833–1883)

The account of the creation in Genesis, although poetically beautiful, had to give way to science.

THE UNCONQUERED!

"Invictus" is a poem to fit the poet. As a boy, W. E. Henley had his leg amputated because of a "tubercular disease of the bone," and in the mid-1800s that must have been a horrific operation. Nevertheless, the disease returned, and Henley had to have the foot of his other leg removed.

And what father or mother cannot also feel Henley's later grief? As an adult, he had to suffer the death of his five-year-old daughter. Yet, Henley, a friend of Robert Louis Stevenson, was never defeated. His was a triumph of the soul!

an is never defeated!

"INVICTUS"

William Ernest Henley (1849–1903):

Out of the night that covers me,
    Black as the Pit from pole to pole,
I thank whatever gods may be
    For my unconquerable soul.

In the fell clutch of circumstance
    I have not winced nor cried aloud.
Under the bludgeonings of chance
    My head is bloody, but unbowed.

Beyond this place of wrath and tears
    Looms but the horror of the shade,
And yet the menace of the years
    Finds, and shall find me, unafraid.

It matters not how strait the gate,
    How charged with punishments the scroll,
I am the master of my fate:
    I am the captain of my soul.

"STONE WALLS DO NOT A PRISON MAKE"

Richard Loveless (1618–1658):

> From "To Althea from Prison"
>
> > Stone walls do not a prison make,
> >   Nor iron bars a cage;
> > Minds innocent and quiet take
> >   That for a hermitage;
> > If I have freedom in my love
> >   And in my soul am free,
> > Angels alone, that soar above,
> >   Enjoy such liberty.

The English poet Richard Lovelace was twice imprisoned for being on the wrong side during political unrest in Britain. Although he was "wealthy, handsome, and of graceful manners," he was reduced to utter poverty and died of consumption in a cellar.

"Grief of the Oceanides at the Fate of Prometheus"

by Charles Lehmann (1814–1882). Said Hemingway, "Man is not made for defeat. A man can be destroyed but not defeated."

Philosophy
A Jewel Without Price

Virtue, Nobility, and Excellence

—the true measures of men and women. Doctrine, Ritual, and Garment—the vanities of the powerful, the measures of the small-minded.

A preface to the good life

Philosophy raises the light of knowledge to the world. Said Voltaire, as only he could,

> In all nations, history is disfigured by fable, till at last philosophy comes to enlighten man; and when it does finally arrive in the midst of this darkness, it finds the human mind so blinded by centuries of error, that it can hardly undeceive it; it finds ceremonies, facts and monuments, heaped up to prove lies.

"THE GREATEST GERMAN OF ALL TIME"

In Johann Wolfgang von Goethe's masterpiece, Faust had so little confidence in the devil's powers that he made a wager:

> If ever I should tell the moment:
> Oh stay! You are so beautiful!
> Then you may cast me into chains,
> then I shall smile upon perdition!

In the meantime, Mephistopheles was to be Faust's servant in all things.

By this theme of a wager, a departure from German folklore, Goethe set his story rolling. Goethe, "the greatest German of all time," borrowed many themes and was able to recast them to create a wondrous work and a very sophisticated devil—a "Lucifer-Mephisto," although in classic demonology, "Mephistopheles" is the name of one of the seven chief devils and the second of the fallen archangels—not Lucifer, himself.

> Since Goethe's death, in 1832, the Faust story, through its various transmutations, has become one of the central myths of the Western world. The theme fascinated composers like Wagner, Schumann, Berlioz, Gounod, Boito, and Mahler, all of whom created important operatic or orchestral scores inspired by Goethe's drama.

We should also include in this list the musical comedy *Damn Yankees.*

PROGRESS FOR PHILOSOPHERS

Christopher Marlowe (1564–1593, age 29!):

In *The Tragedy of Dr. Faustus* (1601), the worldly scholar cries:

> Ugly hell, gape not; come not, Lucifer.
> I'll burn my books. Ah, Mephostophilis!
> [Exeunt with him]

Johann Wolfgang von Goethe (1749–1832):

In *Faust* (1832), the philosopher is saved. The angels say:

> Who ever strives with all his power,
> We are allowed to save.

And thus Faust learns:

> This is the highest wisdom that I own,
> The best that mankind ever knew:
> Freedom and life are earned by those alone
> Who conquer them each day anew.

Two hundred years, then, did result in some progress for philosophers.

MEPHISTOPHELES ON THE TRINITY

Johann Wolfgang von Goethe:

Listen up! The Devil is speaking in Goethe's masterpiece, *Faust*:

> I lost much time on this accursed affliction,
> Because a perfect contradiction
> Intrigues not only fools but also sages.
> This art is old and new, forsooth:
> It was the custom in all ages
> To spread illusion and not truth
> With Three in One and One in Three.
> They teach it twittering like birds;
> With fools there is no intervening.
> Men usually believe, if only they hear words,
> That there must also be some sort of meaning.
> . . . .
> The Church has a superb digestion,
> Whole countries she has gobbled up,
> But is never too full to sup;
> The Church alone has the good health
> For stomaching ill-gotten wealth.

The present writer, of course, does not agree that "the church alone" has been greedy. I have Santayana's tender heart for kindly religion and a profound admiration for all saints. Why, then, quote this irreverence? The Devil made me do it! Perhaps, also, I was still smarting from being boxed about the ears in reading *St. Thomas Aquinas: The Dumb Ox*, by the brilliant Roman Catholic scholar G. K. Chesterton. See page 88 of the present volume.

"Mephistopheles and Faust"
by Alfred Jacomin (1842–1913), a French painter.
Mephistopheles: "For just where no ideas are
the proper word is never far."

THE PASSION OF THE "AUGENBLICK!"

Johann Wolfgang von Goethe:

"O moment stay, thou art so fair!"

As he experiences the *Augenblick*, the ultimate moment, Faust has technically lost his wager with Mephistopheles, who fails to comprehend that Heaven does not run on technicalities. Love and idealism have won the day and robbed "the Devil of a soul." This is a message for fundamentalism, which is always built on legalisms.

The all-encompassing Moment, the *Augenblick*, is not to be found in a search, but comes upon us unexpectedly when we serve others, as in seeking the higher life for the children of the world.

THE PATHOS!

Omar Khayyam (?–1123 C.E.):

Alas, that Spring should vanish with the Rose!
That Youth's sweet-scented Manuscript should close!
The Nightingale that in the Branches sang,
Ah, whence and whither flown again, who knows!

"Rescued From Obscurity"

The Persian poet Omar Khayyam was also learned in the science of his day, but having "failed to find any providence but destiny...he turned to making the most of this life." The Englishman Edward FitzGerald "rescued" the *Rubaiyat* and published his famous translation in 1859.

THERE IS NO LAST HERETIC

As Santayana said in *Reason in Common Sense*: "Reason has the indomitable persistence of all natural tendencies; it returns to attack as waves beat on the shore. To observe its defeat is already to give it new embodiment."

One often refrains from asking the fundamentalists, "Why do the critics of the prophet so often and continually come from former believers? What is there in this great truth that drives good people away who at one time accepted it?"

There is no last heretic in a religion; they are born anew each generation.

He who studies is in great danger of becoming a heretic and ultimately a philosopher, even though in outer things he may appear as most devout.

THE "CONSECRATED ERROR" OF THE PROPHET

George Santayana:

If the idealist fears and deprecates any theory of his own origin and function, he is only obeying the instinct of self-preservation; for he knows very well that his past will not bear examination. He is heir to every superstition and by profession an apologist; his deepest vocation is to rescue, by some logical tour de force, what spontaneously he himself would have taken for consecrated error.... But he detests any admission of relativity in his doctrines, all the more because he cannot avow his reasons for detesting it; and zeal, here as in so many cases, becomes the cover and evidence of a bad conscience. Bigotry and craft, with a rhetorical vilification of enemies, then come to reinforce in the prophet that natural limitation of his interests which turns his face away from history and criticism.

WHERE ST. PAUL WAS WRONG

We cannot agree with the Apostle Paul when he asked, "If after the manner of men I have fought with beasts at Ephesus, what advantageth it me, if the dead rise not? Let us eat and drink, for to morrow we die" (First Corinthians 15:32).

"What!" cried Thomas Huxley in silence as he stood behind the coffin of his little son, "because I am face to face with irreparable loss, because I have given back to the source from whence came, the cause of a great happiness . . . I am to renounce my manhood, and, howling, grovel in bestiality? Why, the very apes know better, and if you shoot their young, the poor brutes grieve their grief out and do not immediately seek distraction in a gorge."

On this point, by that which is good, Paul stands rebuked for despair unworthy of a free man.

AN ANSWER TO PAUL

Matthew Arnold (1822–1888):

Is it so small a thing
To have enjoyed the sun,
To have lived light in the spring,
To have loved, to have thought, to have done;
To have advanced true friends, and
beat down baffling foes? [1]

---

1. Lines from "Empedocles on Etna" (1852). According to legend, Empedocles, the eloquent philosopher of Sicily who flourished around 400 B.C.E., died when he fell into the crater of Mount Etna.

Arnold's intent may not have been to rebuke Paul, as such, but the lines speak for themselves.

"THE SPLENDOR OF MAN'S CAPACITIES"

Thomas H. Huxley:

Thoughtful men, once escaped from the blinding influence of traditional prejudice, will find in the lowly stock whence Man has sprung, the best evidence of the splendor of his capacities; and will discern in his long progress through the Past, a reasonable ground of faith in his attainment of a noble Future.

They will remember that in comparing civilized man with the animal world, one is as the Alpine traveller, who sees the mountains soaring into the sky and can hardly discern where the deep shadowed crags and roseate peaks end, and where the clouds of heaven begin. Surely the awe-struck voyager may be excused if, at first, he refuses to believe the geologist, who tells him that these glorious masses are, after all, the hardened mud of primeval seas, or the cooled slag of subterranean furnaces—of one substance with the dullest clay, but raised by inward forces to that place of proud and seemingly inaccessible glory.

Well said, Mr. Huxley. Well said!

"The Mountain Sprite"

What magic awaits those who climb Huxley's "roseate peaks"—the snows in pink as the slanted light of the sun breaks through the clouds. A mountain sprite or fairy teases the sleeping climber, who carries a crossbow.

Illustration by the German painter Conrad Dielitz (b. 1845)

IN THE MIDST OF SKEPTICISM

Arthur Hugh Clough, an advocate for the cause of higher education for women, served as a professor at Oriel University but eventually resigned because of skepticism. Leaving England, he traveled to the United States in 1852 and visited Emerson.

"Say Not The Struggle Naught Availeth" bears "the mark of spiritual agitation caused by religious doubts," says *The Oxford Companion to English Literature*. When Clough died at age forty-two, Matthew Arnold wrote a commemorating poem, "Thyrsis," which "some critics have ranked among the great English elegies."

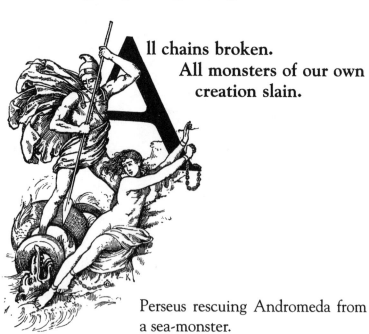

All chains broken.
All monsters of our own creation slain.

Perseus rescuing Andromeda from a sea-monster.

"SAY NOT THE STRUGGLE NAUGHT AVAILETH"

Arthur Hugh Clough (1819–1861):

Say not the struggle naught availeth,
    The labour and the wounds are vain,
The enemy faints not, not faileth,
    And as things have been they remain.

If hopes were dupes, fears may be liars;
    It may be, in yon smoke conceal'd,
Your comrades chase e'en now the fliers,
    And, but for you, possess the field.

For while the tired waves, vainly breaking,
    Seem here no painful inch to gain,
Far back, through creeks and inlets making,
    Comes silent, flooding in, the main.

And not by eastern windows only,
    When daylight comes, comes in the light;
In front, the sun climbs slow, how slowly,
    But westward, look, the land is bright!

A SUMMER REVERIE

Henry David Thoreau (1817–1862):

> I did not read books that first summer; I hoed beans.
> Nay, I often did better than this. There were times
> when I could not afford to sacrifice the bloom of the
> present moment to any work, whether of the head or
> hands. I love a broad margin to my life. Sometimes,
> in a summer morning, having taken my accustomed
> bath, I sat in my sunny doorway from sunrise till
> noon, rapt in revery, amidst the pines and hickories
> and sumaches, in undisturbed solitude and stillness,
> while the birds sang around or flitted noiseless
> through the house, until by the sun falling in at my
> west window, or the noise of some traveller's wagon
> on the distant highway, I was reminded of the lapse
> of time. I grew in those seasons like corn in the
> night, and they were far better than any work of the
> hands would have been. They were not time sub-
> tracted from my life, but so much over and above my
> usual allowance.

Thoreau, author of *On Civil Disobedience*, was a friend
and disciple of Emerson, who leased him the land on
which he built his famous cabin by Walden Pond.

Now here is a summer reverie!

"Washing Venus"
from a painting by Carl Gussow (1843–1907)

What wit, what imagination!

Two fairies engage in a "Fruitless Labor," in an engraving after Rudolf Geyling (b. 1840), a scene fitting Shakespeare's *Midsummer Night's Dream.*

AN ACT OF GOD?

Archbishop Frederick Temple (1821–1902):

"My aunt was suddenly prevented from going a voyage in a ship that went down—would you call that a case of Providential interference?"

"Can't tell; didn't know your aunt."

"A Good Story," the Medicine of Philosophy

ount only the survivors.

It makes for a better story! Yet, in reality, the universe is a very strange place with ample room for coincidence and sheer chance, and fundamentalism doesn't solve any moral problems. On the same day that a ship sinks with 300 people aboard, there will be a person claiming that prayer cured the arthritis in his little finger, or some other thing that is trivial in relation to the evils of the day. This is not to say that the attitude assumed in prayer and meditation is not good for the soul, whether or not the soul is mortal.

Said Jesus, "Sufficient unto the day is the evil thereof" (Matthew 6:34).

NOT A PROFESSOR OF GREEK

Reading some of the titles of Keats's poems—
Endymion, Hyperion, Sonnet To Homer, Hymn To
Apollo, On Seeing The Elgin Marbles, Ode On A
Grecian Urn—the ignorant reader might conclude
that the poet was the product of a special environ-
ment, a cloistered spirit, perhaps the son of an aris-
tocrat or a professor of Greek. But Keats was not
reared in an ivory tower. His father took care of the
horses and cleaned the stalls in his grandfather's liv-
ery stable.

So wrote Louis Untermeyer, and here are some familiar lines from a man who lived but twenty-six years:

"Endymion" (1817)
"A thing of beauty is a joy for ever."

* * *

"On the Grasshopper and the Cricket" (1817)
"The poetry of earth is never dead."

* * *

"Ode to a Nightingale" (1820)
"Already with thee! tender is the night."

* * *

And for a line that summed up the art of Keats's life,
from "Ode On a Grecian Urn" (1820).

"Beauty is truth, truth beauty."

MEAN LITTLE DREAMS

John Keats (1795–1821):

"Fanatics have their dreams, wherewith they weave
A paradise for a sect."

"A DREAM"

John Keats (1795–1821):

Methought I stood where trees of every clime,
Palm, myrtle, oak, and sycamore, and beech,
With plantain,[1] and spice-blossoms, made a screen;
In neighborhood of fountains (by the noise
Soft-showering in my ears), and, (by the touch
Of scent,) not far from roses. Turning round
I saw an arbour with a drooping roof
Of trellis vines, and bells, and larger blooms,
Like floral censers,[2] swinging light in air;
Before its wreathed doorway, on a mound
Of moss, was spread a feast of summer fruits,
Which, nearer seen, seem'd refuse of a meal
By angel tasted or our Mother Eve....

---

1. Plantain: Growing to about fifteen feet, the plantain is crowned with a cluster of broad leaves like a small palm tree. Its fruit must be cooked before eating, and the tourist who mistakes a plantain for a banana will suffer the well-known revenge.

2. censer: a container in which incense is burned.

The island Tauris

in Edmund Kanoldt's "Iphigenia," after Goethe's play "Ephigenia in Tauris." Iphigenia sacrificed all strangers, but one day she discovered that a man she was about to immolate was her brother. She then helped him escape.

FROM THE HEIGHTS TO THE ABYSS

"No other book of mine," said Jack London of *People of the Abyss* (1903), "took so much of my young heart and tears as that study of the poor."

The young socialist, who later wrote *Call of the Wild*, donned the clothes of a poor man and descended into the abyss of the slums of the city of his namesake in England, and in words that could have come from our nightly news, he cries protest across the decades at our own ghettos:

> The mean streets merely look mean from the outside, but inside the walls are to be found squalor, misery, and tragedy....
>
> A new race has sprung up, a *street people*. They pass their lives at work and in the streets. They have dens and lairs into which to crawl for sleeping purposes, and that is all. One cannot travesty the word by calling such dens and lairs "homes."

 an you read without tears, this list of humanity, this list of our children? For shame that it is not a commentary on past ages, but of today.

THE MEASURES OF PHILOSOPHY

Jack London (1876–1916):

> The experience related in this volume fell to me in the summer of 1902. I went down into the underworld of London with an attitude of mind which I may best liken to that of an explorer. I was open to be convinced by the evidence of my eyes, rather than by the teachings of those who had not seen, or by the words of those who had seen and gone before. Further, I took with me certain simple criteria with which to measure . . . That which made for more life, for physical and spiritual health, was good; that which made for less life, which hurt, and dwarfed, and distorted life, was bad.

When first we hear the measures of philosophy, we are astounded by their simplicity and universal appeal. "You mean," we almost ask, "that there is something besides religion? Why didn't somebody tell me? Why didn't they give me its name? How new and beautiful this word, 'philosophy' "!

"HE CHOSE NOTHING"

George Santayana:

On Shakespeare:

In all this depth of experience, however, there is still wanting any religious image. The Sonnets are spiritual, but, with the doubtful exception of the one quoted above, they are not Christian...for Shakespeare, in the matter of religion, the choice lay between Christianity and nothing. He chose nothing; he chose to leave his heroes and himself in the presence of life and of death with no other philosophy than that which the profane world can suggest and understand.

LIFE IS NOT "A MERE PHANTASMAGORIA"

George Santayana:

Shakespeare could be idealistic when he dreamed, as he could be spiritual when he reflected. The spectacle of life did not pass before his eyes as a mere phantasmagoria. He seized upon its principles; he became wise.... It is all the more remarkable, therefore, that we should have to search through all the works of Shakespeare to find half a dozen passages that have so much as a religious sound....We must marvel at this indifference and ask ourselves what can be the causes of it....

But as a whole we must say that Christianity while it succeeded in expressing itself in painting and in architecture, failed to express itself in any adequate drama.

* * *

In Shakespeare's time and country, to be religious already began to mean to be Puritanical; and in the divorce between the fulness of life on the one hand and the depth and unity of faith[1] on the other, there could be no doubt to which side a man of imaginative instincts would attach himself.

---

1. One is reminded of Emerson's observation on the rituals, words, and miracles of the Old Testament: "The more learning you bring to explain them, the more glaring the impertinence. The more coherent and elaborate the system, the less I like it." See selection on page 125 in the present volume.

"EL CRITICON"

The Spanish Jesuit Baltasar Gracian wrote several books, including *El Criticon*, a novel that analyzed civilization through its effects on a primitive man. Gracian belonged to the cult of "euphuists," those who affected a high-blown style of writing and speaking. But in little bits, how fine!

He notes that it is "just as important to have studied men, as to have studied books." And, "Virtue alone is sufficient unto itself: and it, only, makes a man worth loving in life, and in death, worth remembering."

Eloquence on Evil

"Know what is evil, no matter how worshipped it may be. Let the man of sense not mistake it, even when clothed in brocade, or at times crowned with gold, because it cannot thereby hide its hypocrisy, for slavery does not lose its infamy, however noble the master"

AGELESS PHILOSOPHY

Baltasar Gracian (1601–1658):

> Great men are a part of their times. Not all were born
> into a period worthy of them, and many so born
> failed to benefit by it; some merited a better century,
> for all that is good does not always triumph; fashions
> have their periods and even the greatest virtues,
> their styles; but the philosopher has one advantage,
> he is ageless; and should this not prove his century,
> many to follow will.

THE EYE OF FAITH

William H. Prescott (1796–1859):

During an early battle with the Indians of Mexico, some Spaniards claimed to have seen Saint Peter, mounted on his gray war-horse, trampling the bodies of the infidels.

> "Cortes supposed it was his own tutelar saint, St. Peter," says Pizarro y Orellana; "but the common indubitable opinion is, that it was our glorious apostle St. James, the bulwark and safeguard of our nation." "Sinner that I am," exclaims honest Bernal Diaz, in a more skeptical vein, "it was not permitted to me to see either the one or the other of the Apostles on this occasion."

Tantara! Tantara!

Prescott also spoke of "a writer,—probably a monk of the sixteenth century,—in whom ignorance and dogmatism contend for mastery." What lines! And elsewhere on Archbishop Lorenzana's opinion that an icon of the Virgin Mary survived the sacking of Tenochtitlan (Mexico City) by the Spanish: "But the more difficult to explain, the more undoubted the miracle."

"Yet, where there is most doubt, there is often the most dogmatism."

* * *

On the hanging of four hundred Indians by the Spanish: "It was the just recompense of rebellion; a word that has been made the apology for more atrocities than any other word—save religion."

FROM OUT OF A DREAM!

Bernal Diaz del Castillo (1492?–1581):

[We then] arrived at the causeway of Iztapalapa. . . . [and] beheld the number of populous towns on the water and firm ground, and that broad causeway, running straight and level to the city, we could compare it to nothing but the enchanted scenes we had read of in *Amadis of Gaul*,[1] from the great towers and temples, and other edifices of lime and stone which seemed to rise out of the water. To many of us it appeared doubtful whether we were asleep or awake; nor is the manner in which I express myself to be wondered at, for it must be considered, that never yet did man see, hear, or dream of anything equal to the spectacle which appeared to our eyes this day.

When we approached Iztapalapa, we were received by several great lords of that country, relations of Montezuma, who conducted us to our lodgings there, in palaces magnificently built of stone, and the timber of which was cedar, with spacious courts, and apartments furnished with canopies of the finest cotton. After having contemplated these noble edifices we walked through the gardens, which were admirable to behold from the variety of beautiful and aromatic plants, and the numerous alleys filled with fruit trees, roses, and various flowers. . . . When I beheld the scenes that were around me, I thought within myself that this was the garden of the world!

---

1. A famous romance of Spain and Portugal

WHAT PROFIT A MAN TO READ ARISTOTLE?

Aristotle, whom Dante described as the "master of those who know," fell out of favor in the Renaissance through no fault of his own. This famous student of Plato had reasoned that the Earth was at the center of a series of perfect spheres, each with various perfectly round and smooth heavenly bodies, including the Sun. Aristotle's advancement of this theory was an error made into a catastrophe by later Christian readers of Aristotle. When it became Church doctrine, all questioning ceased and so did the advance of astronomy, which had to fight against the church in every step it took from Copernicus to Galileo. Yet Aristotle seems a much different man from the one crammed down the throats of medieval scholars. Observed Louise Ropes Loomis, in her introduction to Aristotle's *On Man in the Universe*:

> He was both a great thinker and a great experimental scientist. Of certain of his own conclusions he said that the facts apparently supported them; but "I say apparently, for the actual facts are not yet sufficiently made out. Should further research ever discover them, we must yield to their guidance rather than to that of theory; for theories must be abandoned, unless their teachings tally with the indisputable results of observation."

Aristotle, "in whom it pleased Nature to try how great a portion of reason she could admit into mortality."

"THE GOLDEN MEAN"

Aristotle (384–322 B.C.E.):

Thus it is possible to go too far, or not far enough in fear, pride, desire, anger, pity, and pleasure and pain generally, and the excess and the deficiency are alike wrong; but to feel these emotions at the right times, for the right objects, towards the right persons, for the right motives, and in the right manner, is the mean or the best good, which signifies virtue.[1]

---

1. For Aristotle, death was the end of the individual, since it dissolved the union of soul and body.

"THE ARTS OF PEACE"

Aristotle:

The charge which Plato brings, in the Laws, against the intention of the Spartan lawgiver, is likewise justified. The whole constitution [of Sparta] aims at creating one kind of virtue only—the virtue of the soldier, which gives victory in war. And so long as they were at war, their power was preserved, but when they had attained empire they fell, for the arts of peace they knew nothing, and had never engaged in any employment higher than war.

O WILD white Bird, faint fluttering
That comes to bid good morrow,
My aching heart doth leap and sing
Forgetful of its sorrow;
I hold thee, little fluttering thing,
Against the heart thou mak'st to spring—
Sweet sister Bird, thy brother mate
May never more be desolate.

Alas! but thou hast made me weep,
Made vacant all the fields of sleep,
For very agony mine eyes
Tell yet of past expectances;
For lo! when o'er my drownèd sight
Thou'lightedst from thy happy flight,
The golden time grew fair again,
I saw the limitless domain
Of Love, where late I walked with thee,
Sweet angel of my agony.

Dear blessèd Bird, thy olive bough
Is salt with tears, and yet I know
The passion of truth and love that sent
Thee to my darkened firmament;
My kisses make revive thy wings,
My heart triumphant leaps and sings,
The Promisèd Bow resplendent shines
Between the sea and terrene lines,
And through the inconstant waves arise
Love's virginal isles of Paradise.

J. ARTHUR BLAIKIE.

Philosophy forever seeks reconciliation:

"And through the inconstant waves arise
Love's virginal isles of Paradise."

"Reconciliation," a poem by J.A. Blaike

"EARTH IS ENOUGH"

Edwin Markham (1852–1940):

> We men of Earth have here the stuff
> Of Paradise—we have enough!
> We need no other stones to build
> The Temple of the Unfulfilled—
> No other ivory for the doors—
> No other marble for the floors—
> No other cedar for the beam
> And dome of man's immortal dream.
>
> Here on the paths of every-day—
> Here on the common human way
> Is all the stuff the gods would take
> To build a Heaven, to mold and make
> New Edens. Ours the stuff sublime
> To build Eternity in time!

In these words of a deeply religious man, we catch a glimpse of the "highest" of religions, that which Santayana called "nobility and excellence."

Philosophy is ageless, serene, and without fear.
It encompasses believers and nonbelievers, drawing the
lines of Good throughout the world. *Philosophia perennis!*
Philosophy everlasting, seeking the Good and advancing
the Right in this life, on this day.

"BRIGHT ANGELIC WINGS"

William Blake, English artist and poet, turned to religious mysticism early in life. At the age of eight, "he beheld 'a tree filled with angels, bright angelic wings bespangling every bough with stars.'"

Raised in a family of Swedenborgians,[1] as the followers of the Swedish mystic Emanuel Swedenborg were called, Blake came to his mysticism naturally. But even if he wrote, "He who shall teach the child to doubt / The rotting grave shall ne'er get out," Blake was no ordinary Christian. For example, he denied the reality of matter, eternal punishment, and authority.

The "doubt" (above) is best broadly stated and includes depriving a child of his innocence or robbing him of his natural idealism. The weight of the world should never be dropped in a child's lap. "Yes, of course, there is a Santa Claus and a tooth fairy! As for God and the afterlife, people believe two things." Both philosophy and religion should be a product of maturity, not force at an early age. Good example, need it be said, is the best teacher.

---

1. Interestingly, Swedenborg taught that heaven was a very solid place, complete with stores, merchandise, schools, and even marriage with sex! This good idea became part of the doctrine of the Church of New Jerusalem, which came to the United States in 1798. Later, Swedenborg's solid sexual heaven was also incorporated into Mormonism's "marriage for time and eternity."

"AUGURIES OF INNOCENCE"

William Blake (1757–1827):

> To see a World in a Grain of Sand,
> And a Heaven in a Wild Flower,
> Hold Infinity in the palm of your hand,
> And Eternity in an hour.

Such a great mind! As one editor said, Blake was "against every conception of God as an omnipotent person, as a body, as a Lord who sets in train any lordship over man." He was "against all accepted Christianity" and "against the churches" and "against priesthood," as well as being against "all theological casuistry that excuses pain and admits evil; against sanctimonious apologies for injustice."

Hear, hear, Mr. Blake! Philosophy forgives your famous:

> Mock on, mock on, Voltaire, Rousseau;
> Mock on, mock on, 'Tis all in vain.
> You throw the sand against the wind.
> And the wind blows it back again.

In another stanza, Blake inaccurately placed the orthodox genius Isaac Newton with the skeptics.

MAN, THE WONDER

Sophocles (496?–406 B.C.E.):

> Many are the wonders of the world
> And none so wonderful as Man.

How curious that three of the monuments of world literature—Sophocles' *Oedipus Rex*, Shakespeare's *Hamlet*, and Dostoyevsky's *The Brothers Karamazov*—deal with the subject of the murder of a father by a son.

The wonder of the world!

We seek religious miracles and fail to see the miracle of
the world before our very eyes. "Benito's Island Home,"
an illustration by True Williams for his novel *Frank Fairweather's Fortunes* (1895).

BEHOLD THE IMMENSITY!

Camille Flammarion (1842–1925):

> Like a shower of stars the worlds whirl, borne along by the winds of heaven, and are carried down through immensity; suns, earths, satellites, comets, shooting stars, humanities, cradles, graves, atoms of the infinite, seconds of eternity, perpetually trans-form beings and things; all move on, all wing their flight under the breath divine—while trade goes on, or the investor counts his gold and piles it up, believing that he holds the entire universe in his casket.[1]

On the other hand, we should not make human insignificance the centerpiece of our philosophy. In a single breath, after all, it is the human mind that beholds this "immensity" and measures it with light years, and light infinities if necessary, and in the next breath, it smiles at the beauty of a spring flower. Then, incomprehensibly, it skips over its own death to a satisfying vision of a future world free from pollution, wars, poverty, and disease. In short, it is in awe, not fear, that we study the immensity, laughing at times at how easily the whole universe fits into the human brain with room to spare. We people of earth are irrepressible in our curiosity and optimism.

---

1.   Flammarion, a French astronomer, popularized the study of astronomy with his many books.

PROPORTION

Percy Bysshe Shelley (1792–1822):

"Ozymandias"

I met a traveler from an antique land
Who said: Two vast and trunkless legs of stone
Stand in the desert. Near them, on the sand,
Half sunk, a shattered visage lies, whose frown,
And wrinkled lip, and sneer of cold command,
Tell that its sculptor well those passions read
Which yet survive, stamped on these lifeless things,
The hand that mocked them, and the heart that fed:
And on the pedestal these words appear:
'My name is Ozymandias, King of Kings:
Look on my works, ye Mighty, and despair!'
Nothing beside remains. Round the decay
Of that colossal wreck, boundless and bare
The lone and level sands stretch far away.[1]

---

1. "Ozymandias" (1817). Note the date of this poem about Egypt. All Europe had taken renewed interest in the land of the pharaohs since Napoleon's conquest of Egypt in 1798. Traveling shows displaying mummies, statues, and papyri toured the Continent and the United States. The hieroglyphics had not yet been translated (Champion, 1821).

"THE GOOD THINGS OF THE MIND"

Francis Bacon (1516–1626):

> For Divinity says, "Seek ye first the kingdom of God, and all these things shall be added to you;" and philosophy says something like it, "Seek ye first the good things of the mind, and the rest will either be supplied, or their loss will not be felt."

Odd it is that we keep coming back to two views of the universe, and here we must repeat Santayana, the atheist:

> Experience has repeatedly confirmed that well-known maxim of Bacon's, that "a little philosophy inclineth man's mind to atheism, but depth in philosophy bringeth men's mind about to religion". . . .
>
> At the same time, when Bacon penned the sage epigram we have quoted he forgot to add that the God to whom depth in philosophy brings back men's minds is far from being the same from whom a little philosophy estranges them.

Such is the irony of truth.

Having considered the great questions, let us go on an adventure.

In the twinkling of an eye, we are off! Look carefully, the door to the castle is open. *The Classic and the Beautiful from the Literature of Three Thousand Years* (1891).

"AN OPPONENT OF LIBERALISM"

Although William Wordsworth's "later writings show him in politics converted from a revolutionist to an opponent of liberalism," it was his poetry that counted, and it was his poetry that survived and left its rainbow in the world. Wordsworth, as Louis Untermeyer writes, was the champion "of the 'humble and rustic life' in which 'the essential passions of the heart find a better soil.'" His was a reaffirmation of "the unity of all life—and even death—with nature."

"MY HEART LEAPS UP WHEN I BEHOLD"

William Wordsworth (1770–1850):

> My heart leaps up when I behold
>   A rainbow in the sky:
> So was it when my life began;
> So is it now I am a man;
> So be it when I grow old,
>   Or let me die!
> The Child is father of the Man;
> And I could wish my days to be
> Bound each to each by natural piety.[1]

---

1. And nice it is to return home, or as Wordsworth said in "Lucy:"

   > I traveled among unknown men,
   > In lands beyond the sea;
   > Nor, England! did I know till then
   > What love I bore to thee.

"THE TELLER OF TALES"

Scotland's Robert Louis Stevenson was a constant traveler in search of a climate to suit his history of ill health, and when one of his voyages took him to the South Pacific, he finally found a home in Samoa. The natives acknowledged him as chief with the name "Tusitala," or the "teller of tales," a perfect description of the author of *Treasure Island* (1883), *Dr. Jekyll and Mr. Hyde* (1886), and *Kidnapped* (1886).

Stevenson, also an essayist and poet, inspired another famous author of adventure stories. In 1885 at the age of twenty-five, H. Rider Haggard made a bet with his brother that he could write a story as good as *Treasure Island.* Six weeks later Haggard completed *King Solomon's Mines.*

"REQUIEM"

Robert Louis Stevenson (1850–1894):

> Under the wide and starry sky,
> Dig the grave and let me lie.
> Glad did I live and gladly die,
> And I laid me down with a will.
>
> This be the verse that you grave for me:
> Here he lies where he longed to be;
> Home is the sailor, home from the sea
> And the hunter home from the hill.

At the age of forty-four, Stevenson died in his beloved Samoa, and the "Requiem" he had written was placed on his tombstone.

"AN INLAND VOYAGE"

One normally thinks of sea adventures such as *Treasure Island* when Robert Louis Stevenson comes to mind, but Stevenson also wrote of his own travels, which were many. He traveled, for example, to Europe and took a canoe tour through Belgium and France, recording it in *An Inland Voyage* (1878). In the same year, he told of his *Travels with a Donkey in the Cevennes* of France.

Having married Mrs. Osbourne in 1880 in America, Stevenson wound up in California and wrote *The Silverado Squatters* (1883). But Stevenson was also a remarkable poet:

> Go, little book, and wish to all
> Flowers in the garden, meat in the hall,
> A bin of wine, a spice of wit,
> A house with lawns enclosing it,
> A living river by the door,
> A nightingale in the sycamore!

A frontispiece for Stevenson's *An Inland Voyage*

Pan rests in some reeds as two canoes pass on a river.

> All wild places were [Pan's] home, thickets and forests and mountains....Upon his pipes of reed he played melodies as sweet as the nightingale's song. He was always in love with one nymph or another, but always rejected because of his ugliness.
>
> Sounds heard in the wilderness at night by the trembling traveler were supposed to be made by him, so that it is easy to see how the expression "panic" fear arose.[1]

---

1. Edith Hamilton speaking of Pan. Note "Arethysa" and "Cigarette," the names of the canoes used by Stevenson.

In this scene with Pan,

the Nymphs are pulling the ugly satyr into the water.

"Satyr and Nymphs," by William Bouguereau (1825–1905), a French painter.

"THE TRUE RELIGION"

Mark Twain (Samuel Clemens, 1835–1910):

"Man is the Religious animal. He is the only Religious Animal. He is the only animal that has the True Religion —several of them."

EVOLUTION AND THE SEA

Carl Sandburg (1878–1967):

> The sea is nothing to look at
> unless you want to know something
> unless you want to know
> where you came from.

On evolution, it is worth noting that the salts found in blood plasma resemble the proportions of the same salts that occur in modern seawater. Further, the unity of life is shown in the fact that 99 percent of all living matter—from amoebas, to plants, to man—is made up mainly of four elements—carbon, hydrogen, oxygen and nitrogen, and that a single building block (DNA) is the basis for all life. Independent of these facts is the fossil record, which always occurs in the correct evolutionary order, except where a layer of earth is folded over. Then trilobites are found on their backs, and large stones, in defiance of gravity, are seen at the top of the layer.

It is a singular curiosity that evolution, an observable fact of nature, could be rejected for so long; yet, sooner or later, the pamphlet that is "creation science" must be measured against the library that is evolution. Every creationist should read Martin Gardner's "Geology Versus Genesis," a chapter in his splendid book *Fads and Fallacies in the Name of Science.*

"MAN WILL YET WIN"

Carl Sandburg (1878–1967):

From "The People, Yes"

Man is a long time coming.
Man will yet win.
Brother may yet line up with brother:

This old anvil laughs at many broken hammers.
    There are men who can't be bought.
    The fireborn are at home in fire.
    The stars make no noise.
    You can't hinder the wind from blowing.
    Time is a great teacher.
    Who can live without hope?

In the darkness with a great bundle of grief
    the people march.
In the night, and overhead a shovel of stars for
    keeps, the people march:

                "Where to? what next?"

"THE LORD HATH DELIVERED HIM INTO MINE HANDS"

During a debate at Oxford in 1860, Bishop Wilberforce spoke for a "full half hour" and then "with smiling insolence, he begged to know, was it through [Huxley's] grandfather's or grandmother's side that he claimed his descent from a monkey?" Turning to a friend, Huxley remarked: "The Lord hath delivered him into mine hands," and he arose and gave his famous and eloquent rebuttal to the Oxford bishop.

Said one man: "No one doubted his meaning, and the effect was tremendous. One lady fainted and had to be carried out; I, for one, jumped out of my seat." Another wrote: "The retort was so justly deserved, and so inimitable in its manner, that no one who was present can ever forget the impression that it made."

THE FAMOUS REPLY

Thomas H. Huxley (1825–1895):

I assert—and I repeat—that a man has no reason to be ashamed of having an ape for his grandfather. If there were an ancestor whom I should feel shame in recalling, it would rather be a man—a man of restless and versatile intellect—who, not content with an equivocal success[1] in his own sphere of activity, plunges into scientific questions with which he has no real acquaintance, only to obscure them by an aimless rhetoric, and distract the attention of his hearers from the real point at issue by eloquent digressions and skilled appeals to religious prejudice.

Mr. Huxley might well also have noted that the Age of Faith—that thousand years from the fall of Rome to the fifteenth century—is gone, and no revival, however successful, and no missionary enterprise, however well-planned and funded, will ever bring it back. Indeed, we can never go home again to those simpler times when the sun and all the stars of Heaven revolved around the earth.

---

1. It is always quoted "equivocal success," but Huxley said he didn't remember using "equivocal."

A PRAYER ADDRESSED TO NO PERSONAL GOD

Jerome Nathanson (1908–1975, quoting Eusebius):

"May I be no man's enemy, and may I be the friend of that which is eternal and abides....May I never devise evil against any man; if any devise evil against me, may I escape...without the need of hurting him. May I love, seek, and attain only that which is good. May I wish for all men's happiness and envy none....When I have done or said what is wrong, may I never wait for the rebuke of others, but always rebuke myself until I make amends....May I win no victory that harms either me or my opponent....May I reconcile friends who are wroth with one another. May I, to the extent of my power, give all needful help...to all who are in want. May I never fail a friend in danger....May I respect myself....May I always keep tame that which rages within me....May I never discuss who is wicked and what wicked things he has done, but know good men and follow in their footsteps."

No, this is not the prayer of a Catholic priest, a Protestant minister, a Jewish rabbi, a Quaker teacher. These words are those of Eusebius, a "pagan" who lived some two thousand years ago. In these words is the voice of man's best hope on earth.

Jerome Nathanson was a prominent American advocate of humanism.

Eusebius was a late Greek Platonist (a follower of Plato), about whom almost nothing is known, not even the date at which he lived!

"EVERY CRADLE ASKS"

Robert Ingersoll (1833–1899):

"Every cradle asks us, 'Whence?' and every coffin, 'Whither?' The poor barbarian weeping above his dead, can answer these questions just as well as the robed priest of the most authentic creed."

"Geni Guarding the Secret of the Tomb"
A sculpture by Rene de Saint-Marceaux (1845–1915)

"HIS MOUNTAIN BELLY AND ROCKY FACE"

"He was a heavy man," said modern critic Robert M. Adams. "Everyone felt it, and he said so himself, heavily. What other lover, in the course of recommending himself to his mistress, ever took occasion to remind her of his mountain belly and rocky face?"

But Ben Jonson's honesty was not appreciated by everyone. He accused the long-winded Puritans, the chant-speaking "sanctified elders," of going to school to learn to talk through their noses: "He has no gift," says Lovewit in the *Alchemist* (1610), "Of teaching in the nose that e'er I knew of." The fanatical Puritans, who felt that even the word "Christmas" was bad,[1] eventually fled to America. Our Pilgrims preferred the Old Testament to the New, and they often called their enemies pagans, Philistines, Canaanites, and even gentiles. They even thought that Hebrew was a better language than English and went to the extreme of avoiding the common names of the months of the calendar, since they were pagan— August, for example, came from "Augustus" Caesar.

Puritan denunciations of the Church of England led to their persecution, their rhetoric against it almost matching their invectives against the Catholic Church, "the rags and tatters of Rome."

---

1. The "mass" in "Christmas" being popish or heathen, they used the words "Nativity" or "Christ-tide."

WISDOM MOST RARE

Ben Jonson (1573–1637):

It is not growing like a tree
In bulk, doth make man better be;
Or standing long an oak, three hundred year,
To fall a log at last, dry, bald, and sere:[1]
    A lily of a day
    Is fairer far in May,
Although it fall and die that night;
It was the plant and flower of light.
In small proportions we just beauties see;
And in short measures life may perfect be.

---

1. sere: dried up, withered.

"LIMPID GRACE"

"As a man Jonson was arrogant and quarrelsome, but fearless, warm-hearted, and intellectually honest." In his 1616 play *The Devil is an Ass*, Ben Jonson ridiculed the "projectors," the pretended demoniacs and witch-finders of his day. Yet, in this fat poet, playwright, and competitor of Shakespeare, we find some of the sweetest lines ever written.

"Readers are continually discovering the limpid grace and quiet pathos of the songs in Jonson's masques [1] and plays." And take these few lines from "To Celia" as a delightful rediscovery:

> Drink to me only with thine eyes,
>   And I will pledge with mine;
> Or leave a kiss but in the cup
>   And I'll not look for wine.
> The thirst that from the soul doth rise
>   Doth ask a drink divine;
> But might I of Jove's nectar [2] sup,
>   I would not change for thine.

---

1. masque: as in masquerade, an old form of drama.

2. Jove's nectar: the death-overcoming drink of the gods. From "Sejanus" (by Jonson): "Twas only fear first in the world made gods."

And from "To the Memory of My Beloved Master William Shakespeare": "He was not of an age, but for all time!"

"The indiscreet soubrette"

or lady's maid, especially one involved in intrigue. What lover has sent these flowers? A love note quoting Ben Jonson, "Drink to me only with thine eyes"? And will the maid tell the woman's husband?

A French painting by Jules Emile Saintin (b. 1829)

IN PRAISE OF EDITH HAMILTON

When *The Greek Way* appeared in 1930, "it immediately fired the imagination of both scholars and general readers. The book is no less exciting today. It communicates the pent-up ardor of a teacher who never became bored with her subject, never let her affection stagnate in petty pedantry. It lures; never lectures. It guides, never patronizes."

And as Oxford's Sir Maurice Bowra continued: "She stood in the noble tradition of humanism in being able to get the best out of the past without losing herself in it, to enrich it with her own wise and percipient observations and to assess it by generous standards of human worth and potentialities."

Edith Hamilton, the "great lady of humanistic letters," lived to age ninety-six. She was a pioneer, being the first woman student admitted to the University of Munich, and later in 1896, she became headmistress of the Bryn Mawr School in Baltimore. At a time when women were still just beginning to challenge male bastions, Edith Hamilton made a great contribution to scholarship that has stood the test of time. And such fine style: "'Excellence,' said Aristotle, 'much labored for by the race of men.'"

"TRUTH IS A JEALOUS MISTRESS"

Edith Hamilton (1867–1963):

Before Greece the domain of the intellect belonged to the priests. They were the intellectual class of Egypt. Their power was tremendous. Kings were subject to it. Great men must have built up that mighty organization, great minds, keen intellects, but what they learned of old truth and what they discovered of new truth was valued as it increased the prestige of the organization. And since Truth is a jealous mistress and will reveal herself not a whit to any but a disinterested seeker, as the power of the priesthood grew and any idea that tended to weaken it met with cold reception, the priests must fairly soon have become sorry intellectuals, guardians only of what seekers of old had found, never using their own minds with freedom.

"THE REPUBLIC OF LETTERS"

Edith Hamilton:

"A great French scholar of the last century said to his class at the College de France shortly after Sedan[1] and the triumphant occupation of Paris by the German army:

> Gentlemen, as we meet here today we are in a free country, the republic of letters, a country which has no national boundaries, where there is neither Frenchman nor German, which knows no prejudice nor intolerance, where one thing alone is valued, truth in all her manifold aspects. I propose to study with you this year the works of the great poet and thinker, Goethe.

How noble and how tranquilizing. The eternal perspectives open out, clear and calm. Intolerance, hatred—how false they look and how petty."

---

1. The French were defeated in 1870 at Sedan, France, by the Prussians.

Nobility
never loses sight of her
target of the higher life
for all of humanity. She
is blind to color, race,
and religion. Her arrow
is forever to the mark.
Such is the dream of
Philosophy!

"A DOUBTER, AN UNDOGMATIC MAN"

Marcus Tullius Cicero, the Roman philosopher, is famous for his essay "On Old Age," which, interestingly, Thomas Jefferson read once each year. But Cicero's importance extends far beyond a single essay. Voltaire described Cicero's *The Nature of the Gods* and the *Tusculan Disputations* as "the two noblest works that ever were penned by mere human wisdom."

Cicero chose to believe in life after death "for the belief makes me happy," but he was "a doubter, an undogmatic man." His influence extended from St. Augustine to Dante, who used Cicero's classification of sins in *The Inferno*, and beyond. His essay "On Duties," Michael Grant writes, "has perhaps exercised more influence on the thought and standards of the Western world than any other secular work ever written."

THE LIFE OF REASON

Marcus Tullius Cicero (106–43 B.C.):

> True Law is Reason, right and natural, commanding
> people to fulfil their obligations and prohibiting and
> deterring them from doing wrong. Its validity is uni-
> versal; it is immutable and eternal. Its commands and
> prohibitions apply effectively to good men, and those
> uninfluenced by them are bad. Any attempt to super-
> sede this law, to repeal any part of it, is sinful; to can-
> cel it entirely is impossible. Neither the Senate nor
> the Assembly can exempt us from its demands; we
> need no interpreter or expounder of it but ourselves.
> There will not be one law at Rome, one at Athens,
> or one now and one later, but all nations will be sub-
> ject all the time to this one changeless and everlast-
> ing law.

Cicero gave the authorship of the "Law" to God, but
other philosophers have given it to "Nature." Yet the
issue remains the same. Socrates (470?–399 B.C.E.), who
believed in God and the afterlife, said this:

> "For our discussion is on no trifling matter,
> but on the right way to conduct our lives."

It was Athens' "sin against philosophy" that Socrates
was forced to drink hemlock, having been falsely accused
of corrupting the youth.

> But neither did I think that I ought, for the sake of
> avoiding danger, to do anything unworthy of a free-
> man.... [for] there are many devices in every danger,
> by which to avoid death, if a man dares to do and say
> anything.

"AN EPITAPH FIT FOR AN OX"

Marcus Tullius Cicero:

Indeed, a life so wholly lacking in reason and moderation must of necessity be highly unattractive. That was the mistake of Sardanapalus, the enormously wealthy king of Syria, who had these lines engraved on his tomb: "Everything that I have eaten, everything I have consumed to satisfy my appetites, is still within my power: all my other great riches I have left behind me, and they are gone." That, remarked Aristotle, is an epithet fit for an ox, not a king. For Sardanapalus claims, in death, to control things which even when he was alive he only possessed at the very moment of enjoyment.

As we read the pagan philosophers, we are reminded of Jacob Bronowski's great lines on Erasmus, the Dutch humanist.

In the Middle Ages the ladder of promotion was through the Church...[but]...at the end of the ladder is always the image, the icon of the godhead that says, "Now you have reached the last commandment: Thou shalt not question."

...But the monk's life was for Erasmus an iron door closed against knowledge. Only when Erasmus read the classics himself, in defiance of orders, did the world open for him. "A heathen wrote this to a heathen," he said, "yet it has justice, sanctity, truth. I can hardly refrain from saying 'Saint Socrates, pray for me!'"

IN PRAISE OF PHILOSOPHY!

Marcus Tullius Cicero:

"No praise, then, is too great for philosophy!—which enables this period [old age] in her obedient disciples lives, like every other period, to be lived without anxiety."

These words were written after the death of Cicero's beloved daughter and after his political banishment. Soon the Triumvirate in Rome, having overwhelmed the republican cause, would arrange for the death of Cicero. They would cut off the head and hands of the man who had written the Philippics in defense of the republic. Cruelty is often the backdrop for the triumph of philosophy.

A CHANGE IN DOCTRINE

In 1633, Galileo was summoned before the Inquisition in Rome and forced to recant his defense of the theory of Copernicus (c. 1530) that the Earth went around the Sun, not vice versa as taught by the Roman Catholic Church. Faced with the threat of the rack, Galileo recanted; yet as he walked away, he mumbled, "But still it moves."

Galileo justified his views by appealing for a nonliteral interpretation of the scriptures. His arguments failed to persuade the clerics, but oddly as history goes, the essence of Galileo's views became the official doctrine of the Church after Pope Leo XIII's encyclical of 1893, *Providentissimus Deus*.

Unwilling to suffer such extreme embarrassment twice, the Catholic Church has been very cautious about making any comment on evolution. As science writer Martin Gardner notes, it is "the increasingly popular Catholic view" that there was "an infusion of soul into a body which had bestial parents."

A PROPHECY FOR EVOLUTION

Galileo Galilei (1564–1642):

"It is surely harmful to souls to make it a heresy to believe what has been proved."

The Devil in Goethe's *Faust* was even more specific in his advice to fundamentalists, and well they have followed it!

> Have but contempt for reason and for science,
> Man's noblest force spurn with defiance,
> Subscribe to magic and illusion,
> The Lord of Lies aids your confusion.

THE EMPEROR SPEAKS

Marcus Aurelius (121–180 C.E.):

"Be not unhappy, or discouraged, or dissatisfied, if you do not succeed in acting always by the right principles; but when you have failed, try again. . . . For thus you will not fail to obey reason, and will find rest in it. And remember that philosophy requires only the things which your nature requires."

* * *

"Simple and modest is the work of philosophy."

* * *

"What then is there which can guide a man? One thing and only one, philosophy."

* * *

"In a word, if there is a god, all is well; and if chance rules, be not you too governed by it."

* * *

"And if you strive to live only what is really your life, that is, the present—then you will be able to pass that portion of life which remains for you up to the time of your death, free from perturbations, nobly, and obedient to your own deity within."

* * *

"While you live, while it is in your power, be good." [1]

* * *

"No man can rob us of our free will."

---

1. Marcus Aurelius, *Meditations*. Marcus Aurelius did not believe that the soul continued to live after death, but was "transmuted and diffused, and turned into fire and absorbed into the creative intelligence of the universe."

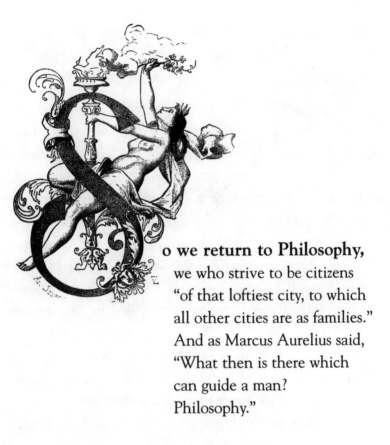

o we return to Philosophy,
we who strive to be citizens
"of that loftiest city, to which
all other cities are as families."
And as Marcus Aurelius said,
"What then is there which
can guide a man?
Philosophy."

WE, THE VOYAGERS

Henry Beston:

"For a moment of night we have a glimpse of ourselves and of our world islanded in its stream of stars—pilgrims of mortality, voyaging between horizons across eternal seas of space and time."

To make such a discovery, to come upon such a line, is the delight of philosophy. After considering some lines from Lucian's *Icaromenippus, An Aerial Expedition* (c. 100 B.C.E.), the present editor was thumbing through Bartlett's for a selection to fit Doré's engraving of "A Voyage to the Moon" and found this quotation from *The Outermost House: A Year of Life on the Great Beach of Cape Cod* (1928). Thus, I was led on a quest for a book and in the process learned something of this man Henry Beston, whose name is not in my one-volume *Webster's Biographical Dictionary*.

What joy it is to be a treasure hunter through the world of literature and ideas! Shores upon shores, growing, limitless, this continent of the mind!

Said the great Edith Hamilton, " 'Beyond the last peaks and all seas of the world' stands the serene republic of what Plato calls 'the fair and immortal children of the mind.' "

"A Voyage to the Moon"

In *Baron Munchausen, Narrative of His Marvellous Travels* (1758), the Baron's ship is seized by a hurricane and swept up a thousand leagues, sailing above the clouds for six weeks until it arrives at the moon. Engraving by Doré.

OH BEAUTIFUL LALLA ROOKH

The Persian poet in "Lalla Rookh" was not Omar Khayyam, but the engraving on the next page so captures the spirit of the "Loaf of Bread" quatrain that I had to use it here. Remember the lines of the *Rubaiyat?*

> Here with a Loaf of Bread beneath the Bough,
> A Flask of Wine, a Book of Verse—and Thou
>   Beside me singing in the Wilderness—
> And Wilderness is Paradise enow.

This wonderful engraving (*opposite*) is of "Lalla Rookh," a princess who as she traveled in India fell in love with a young Persian poet. To her delight, she later learned that the poet was the sultan to whom she was betrothed. The story was told by Thomas Moore (1817), who was supposedly a friend of Byron and received the poet's memoirs in trust, but later destroyed them!

The Beautiful Lalla Rookh[1]

---

1. By A. deValentine (1862–1925), an American painter.

"THE SEA OF FAITH"

Some sadness is necessary for depth of soul, and even the most optimistic of philosophers will falter at times. We should beware of people who are so happy that they never stop smiling.

If we are lucky, the worst tragedies will pass us by, and this is not to speak of death, which after a long, full life seems natural enough. Yet, even in great pain, we concede nothing to despair. We must begin again, as Matthew Arnold says, and we agree when he says that: "I am a Liberal, yet I am a Liberal tempered by experience, reflection, and renouncement, and I am, above all, a believer in culture."

SUCH SADLY MAGNIFICENT LINES!

Matthew Arnold (1822–1888):

From "Dover Beach"

The sea of faith
Was once, too, at the full, and round earth's shore
Lay like the folds of a bright girdle furled.
But now I only hear
Its melancholy, long, withdrawing roar,
Retreating, to the breath
Of the night-wind, down the vast edges of drear
And naked shingles of the world.

Ah, love, let us be true
To one another! for the world, which seems
To lie before us like a land of dreams,
So various, so beautiful, so new,
Hath really neither joy, nor love, nor light,
Nor certitude, nor peace, nor help for pain;
And we are here as on a darkling plain
Swept with confused alarms of struggle and flight,
Where ignorant armies clash by night.

"THE LAND WHERE THE LEMON BLOSSOMS BLOW"

Johann Wolfgang von Goethe (1749–1832):

> Know you the land where the lemon blossoms blow,
> And through dark leaves the golden oranges glow,
> A gentle breeze wafts from an azure sky,
> The myrtle's still, the laurel tree grows high—
> You know it, yes? Oh there, oh there
> With you, O my beloved, I would fare.

This song is from Goethe's novel *Wilhelm Meister's Apprenticeship*. When Wilhelm hears Mignon, a waif befriended by Wilhelm, he asks where she learned the song, but Mignon doesn't answer, leaving the mystery of her past unknown.

"Alexis and Dora"

based on a poem by Goethe. An engraving after a work by
Wilhelm von Kaulbach (1805–1874), a German painter.

"ALL WISE MEN HAVE THE SAME RELIGION"

Benjamin Disraeli (1804–1881):

"All wise men have the same religion, but wise men never tell."

This paraphrase is from Disraeli's novel *Endymion* (1880), the story of Endymion's rise from poverty to political power, and Myra, his twin sister, to social eminence.

Endymion comes from the Greek myth in which the goddess Selene (Diana, the moon goddess) became enamored with a sleeping shepherd boy named Endymion. His beauty was so great that she caused him to sleep forever that she might always enjoy his beauty. In another version, Zeus gave Endymion eternal youth and the gift of sleeping as long as he desired.

Adrift in a boat through the gardens of philosophy
The light of an afternoon sun has colored the sky, and we
will soon stop for refreshment. What a day this has been!
It was beauty that first soothed the soul, as love brought
it meaning.

THIS, OUR INHERITANCE

William Shakespeare (1564–1616):

Hamlet is speaking in Act II, scene ii:

> What a piece of work is man! how noble in reason!
> how infinite in faculties! in form and moving how
> express and admirable! in action how like an angel!
> in apprehension how like a god! the beauty of the
> world, the paragon of animals!

Our glorious victory is not in overcoming death, but in overcoming ourselves! Not in our creations of new technology, but in our discovery of philosophy, or if such is our temperament, the higher interpretation of our religion. Though mortal and imperfect, a person may find happiness by cultivating in himself and society those ancient universal measures of worth—virtue (as in the doing of what is right), nobility (as in the vision of a higher life for everyone), and excellence (as in the pursuit of perfection in all things).

Gloria Victis

An engraving after a sculpture by Marius Jean Antonin Mercié (1845–1916)

OF LIES TOLD IN THE WORLD

And now with the sound of trumpets. Tantara! Tantara! Tantara!

The eternal measures of men and women are virtue, nobility, and excellence. They are not now, have not been, and will never be doctrine, ritual, and garment— though these things be praised always by the powers that be. Oh, philosopher, let this be your test: Travel five hundred years into the past, taking with you the true measures of philosophy, and you will be recognized by the men of the past. "I know you. You are a good man," they will say. Travel five hundred years into the future with these things, and you will be at home with the men of the future. Travel with the vanities of the world, and you will be as Moses, "a stranger in a strange land."

This is no idle vision, for we are travelers in mortality and forever at the meridian of human events. Indeed, we are the past, the present, and the future. Thus philosophy declares, "The journey is the goal."

"Time Sustaining Truth"
Need more be said?

Engraving after a work by Nicholas Poussin (1594–1665), a French painter.

THE STANDARD OF PHILOSOPHY

Robert Ingersoll (1833–1899):

"The Humanist Credo"

Justice is the only worship.
Love is the only priest.
Ignorance is the only slavery.
Happiness is the only good.
The time to be happy is now,
The place to be happy is here,
The way to be happy is to make others so.
Wisdom is the science of happiness.

"Time Bringing Truth to Light"

by the Italian artist Federigo Zuccaro (1543–1589). Father
Time is pulling Truth out of the dark clouds of ignorance.

In Imitation of the Classics

NOTES TO QUOTATIONS AND ILLUSTRATIONS

Sources of quotations and illustrations are listed below by page number. The rare books cited here are owned by the author.

ii. "The Fair Venetian," by Titian (1477–1576) from *The Library of Choice Literature*, edited by Ainsworth R. Spofford and Charles Gibbon (Philadelphia: Gebbie and Co., Publishers, 1883), vol. 1, frontispiece.

v. "Introduction" design from *The Art-Journal Illustrated Catalogue of the Universal Exhibition* (Paris, 1867), vol. 7 of *The Art-Journal* (London: London, Virtue, & Co., 1868), p. 282.

vi. "Renown," an engraving from a sculpture by Antonin Mercié in *The Chefs-D'Oeuvre D'Art of the International Exhibition, 1878*, edited by Edward Strahan (Philadelphia: Gebbie & Barrie, Publishers, not dated [1879?], plate facing p. vi.

vii. "Consolation," a reference to Boethius, *The Consolation of Philosophy* (c. 500 A.D.), and other lines in imitation thereof.

viii. "Art and Literature" by William Bouguereau, in *Selected Pictures from the Art Treasures of America*, by Edward Strahan and William Walton (New York: George Barrie, Publisher), vol. 2, facing p. 24.

x. Figure from the "Cabinet of Alessandri and Son," *The Art-Journal Catalogue*, p. 269. See note v.

1. The drawing is taken from the frontispiece of *Great Men and Famous Women*, edited by Charles F. Horne (New York: Selmar Hess, Publisher, 1894). Wording added.

Cicero: Selected Works, edited by Betty Radice, translated by Michael Grant (New York: Penguin Books, 1960), p. 214.

George Santayana, *Soliloquies in England* (New York: Charles Scribner's Sons, 1924), p. 116.

2. Jesse D. Clarkson, *A History of Russia*, (New York: Random House, 1961), p. 361.

3. The quotation is from Aylmer Maude's introduction to his translation of Tolstoy's *On Life and Essays on Religion* (New York: Oxford University Press, World Classics, 1950), p. xvi. Maude did not identify the source of the quotation, adding a mystery to these little-known, but impressive words. They undoubtedly lie buried somewhere in one of Tolstoy's heavy volumes.

Illustration: *Chefs-D'Oeuvre D'Art* (1889), unidentified owl, p. 45. See note vi.

4. Corliss Lamont, *The Philosophy of Humanism* (New York: Frederick Ungar Publishing Co., 1965), p. 46.

5. George Santayana, *Reason in Common Sense*, vol. 1 of *The Life of Reason: or the Phases of Human Progress* (1905, reprint—New York: Dover Publications, 1980), p. 13 and p. 200.

Illustration: unidentified work by Abraham Bloemaert (1564–1651), a Dutch painter, in *The Great Painters of Christendom*, by John Forbes-Robertson (New York: Cassell & Company, Limited, 1877), p. 200.

7. *The First Collected Edition of the Works of Oscar Wilde: 1908–1922*, 15 volumes, edited by Robert Ross (London: Dawsons of Pall Mall, 1969), vol. 3, p. 134. "Lady Windermere's Fan," act III.

X. B. Saintine, *Le Chemin Des Ecoliers* (Paris: Librairie De L. Hachette, 1861), with 450 "vignettes" by "G. Doré, Foster, Etc." The winged horse is by Doré, but the other individual sketches are not always identified. Most seem to be by Paul Gustave Doré (1833–1883), a French artist and famous engraver.

8. *The Life of Man Symbolized by the Months of the Year*, edited by Richard Pigot and illustrated by John Leighton (London: Long-

mans, Green, Reader, and Dyer, 1866), p. ix.

9. *The Poetical Works of Henry Wadsworth Longfellow*, (Boston: Houghton, Mifflin, and Co., 1880), vol. 4, p. 889. Design for Longfellow's "Ultima Thule," engraving by W. J. Dana, E. H. Garrett, artist.

10. Santayana, *Reason in Common Sense*, vol. 1 of *The Life of Reason* (1905), pp. 3, 7, 252. See note 5.

11. Ibid., p. 262.
Illustration: *Le Chemin Des Ecoliers*, p. 580. See note 7.

12. James Spedding, Robert Leslie Ellis, and Douglas Denon Heath, editors, *The Works of Francis Bacon*, vol. 6, new edition (New York: Garret Press, Inc., 1870). Francis Bacon as a boy, frontispiece.
Will Durant, *The Story of Philosophy* (New York: Washington Square Press, 1961), p. 106.

13. *The Essays of Counsels, Civill and Morall* (1625, old spelling). See Francis Bacon, *The Essays*, edited with an introduction by John Pitcher (New York: Penguin Books, 1985), p. 209.

14. David Hume, *An Inquiry Concerning Human Understanding*, introduction by Charles. W. Hendel (New York: Bobbs-Merrill Company, Inc., 1955), p. xviii. Hendel is quoting from an edition of the same work edited by J. M. Keynes and P. Sraffa (Cambridge, 1938).

15. Ibid., "Of Miracles," p. 125.

16. Voltaire quote from Durant, *The Story of Philosophy*, p. 105-106. Poetry by Alexander Pope, "Essay on Man" (1733), in *The Complete Poetical Works of Alexander Pope*, edited by Henry W. Boynton (Houghton Mifflin Company, New York, 1903). See note 12 and 18 (below).

17. Voltaire, *Candide, or Optimism*, edited by Norman L. Torrey (New York: Meredith Publishing Company, 1964), pp. 70 and 22. See also John H. Robertson, *Selected Works of Voltaire* (London: Watts & Co., 1922).

18. Alexander Pope, "Essay on Man" (line 291), in *The Complete Poetical Works of Alexander Pope*, p. 141. Lines quoted in order:

"An Essay on Criticism," part II (p. 70), part II (p. 74), part III (p. 76), "An Essay on Man," Epistle I (p. 139), and Epistle II (p. 142).

19. Ibid., "An Essay on Man," Epistle IV (p. 154).
The Works of Robert Ingersoll (New York: The Dresden Publishing Co, 1893), vol. 1, p. 7 of *The Gods* (1872), and vol. 12, *Miscellany*, p. 352.
Illustration: *The Art-Journal Catalogue*, p. 266. See note v.

20. H. L. Mencken, *A New Dictionary of Quotations* (New York: Alfred A. Knopf, 1942), p. 714.

21. W. H. Milburn, *The Royal Gallery of Poetry and Art* (London: N. D. Thompson Publishing Co., 1886), unidentified engraving of a woman in her library, p. 352.

22. W. Beran Wolfe, *How to be Happy though Human* (New York: Farrar and Rinehart, 1931), p. 257.
Voltaire, *Zadig-L'Ingenu*, translated with an introduction by John Butt (New York: Penguin Books, 1964), p. 21. The wording is slightly different from the version cited by Durant, *The Story of Philosophy*, p. 213. See note 12.

23. Wolfe, *How to be Happy*, 5-6 and p. 360.
"Vanloo," by Francis Boucher (1704–1770), who "did his best to minister to the prurient tastes of a corrupt age." John Forbes-Robertson, editor of *The Great Painters of Christendom*, p. 322-323. See note 5.

24. The Bible (Proverbs 30:18-19).
Illustration: *Le Chemin Des Ecoliers*, p. 412. See note 7.

25. Edward Strahan and William Walton, *Selected Pictures from The Art Treasures of America* (New York: George Barrie, Publisher, 1888), vol. 1, plate after p. 36, "Between Love and Riches."

26. Diogenes Laertius, *Lives of Eminent Philosophers*, translated by R. D. Hicks and introduction by Herbert S. Long (Cambridge, Mass: Harvard University Press, the Loeb Classical Library, 1925, reprinted 1972), vol. 2, book 10, "Epicurus," p. 465

27. Ibid., book 9, "Protagoras, p. 465.
Thucydides, *History of the Peloponnesian War*, translated by Rex

Warner, with an introduction and notes by M. I. Finley (Baltimore, Md: Penguin Books, 1972), introduction (cover) and p. 155.

Illustration: artist not certain, *Le Chemin Des Ecoliers*, p. 227. See note 7.

28. Diogenes Laertius, *Lives of Eminent Philosophers*, vol. 2, p. 41 and vol. 1, introduction by Herbert S. Long, pp. xvii-xviii. See note 26.

29. Ibid., book 6, vol. 2, "Diogenes," p. 41, "Stand out of my light." "Stand from between me and the sun," is from *Webster's Biographical Dictionary* (Springfield, Mass: G. and C. Merriam Company, Publishers, 1980 edition) "Diogenes," p. 421. Translated edition not given.

Illustration: "Diogenes in his Tub," by Jean-Leon Gerome, *Great Men and Famous Women* (1894), vol. 2, p. 44 (facing). See note 1.

30. Translator's note from *Cicero: Selected Works*, edited by Betty Radice, translated with an introduction by Michael Grant, pp. 246-247, "On Old Age." See note 1.

31. Diogenes Laertius, *Lives of Eminent Philosophers*, vol. 2, "Epicurus," p. 651, unidentified quoted version slightly different. See note 26.

G. Santayana, *Reason in Religion*, vol. 3 of *The Life of Reason* (1905), P. 240. See note 5.

Illustration: *Le Chemin Des Ecoliers*, p. 130. See note 7.

32. "Pompeii in Black and White" from an article by Jane E. Harrison about "Euphorion," a poem by F. Gregorvius. Illustration of "Death and Peace," *The Treasury of Art* (New York: Cassell & Co. 1886), p. 104.

Note: There are at least two volumes of *The Treasury of Art* (1886, green cover, and 1883, blue cover, as the present editor distinguishes them), containing issues of the *Magazine of Art*. The volumes are not numbered, nor do they contain publishing data. The dates are approximate.

33. "The Secret," an engraving from a painting by E. Blair Leighton, *The Treasury of Art* (1886), p. 433.

35. *The Chicago Times*, November 14, 1879. See *The Works of Robert G. Ingersoll*, vol. 3, pp. 20-21. See note 19.

"The Death-bed of St. Cecilia," engraving from a painting by

Frans de Vriendt (1517–1570), The Treasury of Art (1883), p. 156. See note 32.

36. Diogenes Laertius, Lives of Eminent Philosophers, vol. 2, book 9, "Protagoras," pp. 469, and vol. 1, introduction, p. xix. See note 26.

37. Ibid., pp. 463-65. Engraving of "The Cellini Salt-Cellar," made of gold, from The Treasury of Art (1883), p. 206. Benvenuto Cellini (1500–1571), a pupil of Michelangelo, was banished from Florence as a result of a duel. See note 32.

38. Thomas Huxley, "The Origin of the Species", an essay in Huxley's Darwiniana (1893, reprint of the McMillan and Company edition—New York: Greenwood Press, Publishers, 1968), pp. 51-52.
"The Infant Hercules," by Sir Joshua Reynolds (1723–1792), The Great Painters of Christendom (1877), p. 374. See note 5.

39. Ibid.

40. John M. Robertson, Voltaire, p. 122. See note 17.
Oliver Wendell Holmes, Jr., The Path of the Law (1897). Found in Bartlett's (p. 787 b), but volume not located.

41. Design from Wilfrid Meynell, Modern Art and Artists (Cassell & Company, Limited, New York, 1888), p. 73.

42. "Kubla Khan, or A Vision in a Dream," in The Portable Coleridge, edited by I. A. Richards (New York: Penguin Books, 1978), p. 157.
Dame Edith Sitwell, ed., The Atlantic Book of British and American Poetry (Boston: Little, Brown and Company, 1958), p. 579.

43. Ibid., "Rime of the Ancient Mariner," part II, p. 85.
Samuel Taylor Coleridge, Aids to Reflection and The Confessions of an Inquiring Spirit: To which are added His Essays on Faith and The Book of Common Prayer, Etc. (London: George Bell and Sons, 1890), p. 66, Aphorism 25.

44. Durant, The Story of Philosophy, p. 149 and p. 154. See note 12.

45. Ibid., p. 149.
Vase of "lapis-lazuli and other precious stones, chiselled, and set

with stones still more precious," by "artist-jewellers," MM. Duron. *The Art-Journal Catalogue*, p. 227. See note v.

46. Corliss Lamont, *The Illusion of Immortality*, introduction by John Dewey (New York: Frederick Ungar Publishing Co., 1965), p. 13 and p. 205.

47. *The Poetical Works of Henry Wadsworth Longfellow* (1880), vol. 2, p. 389. Engraving by A.V.S. Anthony after F.B. Schell for "The Sicilian's Tale." See note 9.

48. *The Incas of Pedro de Cieza de Leon*, translated by Harriet de Onis, edited by Victor Wolfgang von Hagen (Norman, Okla: University of Oklahoma Press, 1959), p. xxvii of Von Hagen's introduction. Illustration in *The Great Painters of Christendom*, p. 265.

49. *The Incas of Pedro de Cieza de Leon*, p. xxxi. Illustration by Doré in *Le Chemin Des Ecoliers*, p. 569. See note 7.

50. Hume, "Essay on Miracles," in *An Inquiry Concerning Human Understanding*, p. 124. See note 14.
Pliny the Elder, *Natural History: A Selection*, translated with an introduction and notes by John F. Healy (New York: Penguin Books, 1991), p. 118.

51. Thomas Huxley, "Agnosticism," an essay in *Science and the Christian Tradition* (D. Appleton and Company, New York, 1897), p. 239. Original source of the second quotation not located.
Marcus Aurelius and His Times, "Lucian of Samosata, Skeptic," introduction by Irwin Edman (New York: Walter J. Black, Inc., Classics Club, 1945), p. 198.

52. Huxley, "Agnosticism," pp. 240-241.

53. "St. Dominic Burning Heretical Books," Giuseppi Maria Mitelli, after Lionello Spada, in *The Illustrated Bartsch*, vol. 42, *Italian Masters of the Seventeenth Century*, edited by John T. Spike (New York: Abaris Books, 1981), p. 297.

56. *The Great Painters of Christendom*, frame from an article about Paul Veronese (c. 1528–1599), p. 122, words added. See note 5.
G. K. Chesterton, *Saint Thomas Aquinas*, *"The Dumb Ox"* (New

York: An Image Book, Doubleday, 1956), p. 106.

57. Santayana, *Reason in Religion*, vol. 3 of *The Life of Reason* (1905), p. 53. See note 5.
Illustration from an article about Giotto di Bondone (1276–1336), a pre-Renaissance Florentine painter. *The Great Painters of Christendom*, p. 26. See note 5.

58. From Voltaire's pamphlet, "We Must Take Sides," *Selected Works of Voltaire*, translated by Joseph McCabe (London: Watts & Co., 1921), p. 18 and p. xiii (introduction).

59. "Pandora," by Arthur Rackham, in Nathaniel Hawthorne, *A Wonder Book* (New York: Garden City Publishing Co., Inc., 1922[?]), a rare book, p. 92 (facing).

60. Louis Untermeyer, *A Concise Treasury of Great Poems* (New York: Simon and Schuster, 1958), commentary on John Donne, p. 100.
Also, *The Oxford Companion to English Literature*, edited by Sir Paul Harvey (New York: Oxford University Press, 1980), p. 243.
Illustration from *Le Chemin Des Ecoliers* (Paris, 1861), p. 516. See note 7.

61. John Donne, "No Man Is An Island," Untermeyer, *A Concise Treasury of Great Poems*, p. 98.
Bell tower from *The Poetical Works of Henry Wadsworth Long-fellow* (Boston: Houghton, Mifflin and Company, 1880), vol. 6, p. 1222. See note 9.

63. "Locksley Hall," in *The Poetical Works of Alfred Tennyson*, illustrated edition (New York: Belford, Clarke & Co., 1884), p. 84.

64. Boethius, *The Consolation of Philosophy*, translated with an introduction by V. E. Watts (New York: Penguin Books, 1969), p. 30. See *The Age of Belief*, edited by Anne Freemantle (New York: The New American Library, 1954), p. 56 and p. 72.

65. Ibid., pp. 40, 65, 39, 38.

66. Ibid., p. 40 and p. 65. Vase by M. Lerolle, who "ranks among the foremost bronze manufacturers of Paris." *The Art-Journal Catalogue*. See note v.

67. Robert Ingersoll in *The Blade*, Toledo, Ohio, January 9, 1892. See "My Belief and Unbelief" in *The Works of Robert G. Ingersoll*, vol. 8, pp. 486-487. See note 19.

68. Spinoza, *Ethics* (completed in 1674, but published, for obvious reasons, after his death). See Benedict de Spinoza, *On the Improvement of the Understanding, The Ethics, and Correspondence*, unabridged, R.H.M. Elwes translation (New York, Dover Publications, Inc., 1955), pp. 78-79. Wording slightly different from the version quoted here by Durant, *The Story of Philosophy*, p. 155.

Spinoza's Ethics and "De Intellectus Emendatione," translated by A. Boyle with an introduction by George Santayana (New York: E. P. Dutton & Company, "Everyman's Library," 1910), p. xxii.

69. "The Philosopher," by Frans Van Mieris (1635–1681), *The Great Painters of Christendom*, p. 224. See note 5.

70. Tennyson, "The Lotos-Eaters," in *The Poetical Works of Alfred Tennyson*, p. 42. See note 63.

71. Homer, *The Odyssey*, translated by W. H. D. Rouse (New York: New American Library, 1937), book v, p. 63.

Homer, *The Odyssey*, translated by E. V. Rieu (Baltimore, Md: Penguin Books, 1946), book vii, p. 118.

72. "The Heroes of the Trojan War," artist not identified, *Great Men and Famous Women*, vol. 3, p. 11. See note 1.

73. "The Judgment of Paris," by H. Peters Gray, in *Selected Pictures*, vol. 2, p. 76. See note 25.

74. Tennyson, "Ulysses," in *The Poetical Works of Alfred Tennyson*, p. 80. See note 63.

75. "The Trojan Horse," by Henri Motte in *Selected Pictures*, vol. 1, p. 108. See note 25.

76. Swinburne, "The Garden of Proserpine" (1866), in *The Major Victorian Poets*, edited by William H. Marshall (New York: Washington Square Press, 1967), p. 707.

Untermeyer, *A Concise Treasury of Great Poems*, commentary on Swinburne, p. 367.

77. A. Tennyson, "In Memoriam," stanza xcvi, *The Poetical Works of Alfred Tennyson*, p. 228. See note 63.
Untermeyer, *A Concise Treasury of Great Poems*, commentary on Tennyson, p. 293-294. See note 60.

78. "The Raven," in *Selected Stories and Poems: Edgar Allan Poe* (New York: Airmont Books, 1962), p. 223.

79. "Murders in the Rue Morgue," in *Selected Stories and Poems: Edgar Allan Poe*, pp. 57-58.

80. James Randi, "Prophecy and the Selling of Nostradamus" and "Nostradamus: The Prophet for All Seasons," *The Skeptical Inquirer* (Fall 1982, published by the Committee for the Scientific Investigation of Claims of the Paranormal), pp. 30-36.
Illustration: Cartoonist Rob Pudim hits the bulls-eye for "Prophecy: The Search for Certainty," an article by Charles J. Cazeau, in the same issue of *The Skeptical Inquirer*.

81. Ibid., p. 33.

82. George Santayana, "The Poetry of Christian Dogma," an essay in *Interpretations of Poetry and Religion* (1900). (Reprint—Gloucester, Mass: Peter Smith, 1969), pp. 108-109.

83. Ibid., p. 108.
Unidentified engraving from the "List of Illustrations," *The Great Painters of Christendom*, p. xi. See note 5.

84. Francois Marie Arouet de Voltaire, "Of the Celibacy of the Clergy," *A Philosophical Dictionary*, ten volumes in one (New York: Coventry House, 1932), pp. 306-307.

85. "The Temptation of St. Antony," engraving from a painting by Aime Nicolas Morot after Adrien Marie, *The Masterpieces of French Art*, (Philadelphia: Gebbie & Co., Publishers, 1882[?]), vol. 2, unpaged portion of the volume.

86. St. Jerome, "Letter to Laeta," *The Library of Christian Classics*, vol. 5, trans. and ed. by S. L. Greenslade (Philadelphia: Westminster, 1956), pp. 341-42; Chesterton, *Aquinas*, pp. 104-105. See note 56.

87. "Temptation," by Henri Guillaume Schlesinger. Review by J. Eugene Reed, editor of The Masterpieces of German Art (Philadelphia: Gebbie & Co., Publishers, 188?, not dated), vol. 1, unpaged portion.

88. Walter Kaufmann, The Faith of a Heretic (New York: Doubleday & Company, Inc., 1961), pp. 75.
G.K. Chesterton, St. Thomas Aquinas, p. 194. See note 56.

89. "Last Supper of the Protestants and the Pope's Descent to Hell," by Lucas Cranach, the younger, in Max Geisberg, The German Single-Leaf Woodcut: 1500–1550, revised by Walter L. Strauss (Hacker Art Books Inc., New York, 1975), vol. 2, p. 618.

90. Julian Huxley, Religion Without Revelation (New York: The New American Library, 1957), pp. 160-161.

91. "The Mesmerist and Mathias," an engraving by Gillott after Adrien Marie, in E. Cobham Brewer, Character Sketches of Romance, Fiction and Drama, edited by Marion Harland (New York: Selmar Hess Publisher, 1892), vol. 3, p. 30 (facing).

92. Oxford Dictionary of Quotations, third edition (Toronto: Oxford University Press, 1980), "William Occam," p. 364.
John Handyside, trans., Kant's Inaugural Dissertation and Early Writings on Space, (Chicago: The Open Court Publishing Company, 1929), p. 83.

93. The Chefs-D'Oeuvre D'Art, engraved letter "Q," from a design by Kaemmerer, p. 112. See note vi.

94. Bertrand Russell, Why I Am Not A Christian (New York: Simon and Schuster, Inc., 1957), cover and p. v.

95. Ibid., p. 9 and pp.13-14. "The Faith of a Rationalist," BBC Radio broadcast quoted by George Seldes in The Great Quotations (Secaucus, N.J.: The Citadel Press, 1983), p. 607.

97. H. G. Wells, The War of the Worlds (1898). See the neat cover of the Airmont Publishing Company edition (New York, 1964), p. 1.

98. Joseph Conrad, Heart of Darkness & The Secret Sharer, intro-

duction by Albert J. Guerard (New York: New American Library, 1950), cover introduction.

99. Conrad, "Youth." *The Golden Argosy: The Most Celebrated Short Stories in the English Language*, edited by Van H. Carmell and Charles Grayson (New York: The Dial Press, 1955), p. 102.

100. Phyllis McGinley, *Times Three: Selected Verse From Three Decades*, with Seventy New Poems, foreword by W. H. Auden (New York: The Viking Press, 1960), pp. 38-39.
Illustration: *Poetical Works of Longfellow*, vol. 5, p. 951.

101. *The Great Painters of Christendom*, p. 32. See note 5.
"The Fairies," by Allingham, in *The Viking Book of Poetry of the English-Speaking World*, edited by Richard Aldington (New York: The Viking Press, 1958), vol. 2, p. 974.

102. William H. Prescott, *The History of the Conquest of Mexico*, abridged and edited by C. Harvey Gardiner (Chicago: Phoenix Books, The University of Chicago Press, 1966), introduction p. xxi and p. xvii.
History of the Conquest of Mexico and *History of the Conquest of Peru* (New York: The Modern Library, current), p. 561. Prescott's footnotes often surpass his text for sheer brilliance, pp. 82-83.

103. Ibid., pp. 69-70, and p. 561 (Modern Library).
Design from *Modern Art and Artists*, p. 88. See note 41.

104. Walt Whitman, "With Antecedents," in *Leaves of Grass*, introduction by Gay Wilson Allen (New York: New American Library, 1955), p. xii.
Untermeyer, *A Concise Treasury of Great Poetry*, commentary on Walt Whitman, p. 339. See note 60.
See also, *A New Dictionary of Quotations*, p. 891. See note 20.
Compare: Whitman, *Leaves of Grass*, p. 206.

105. *The Great Painters of Christendom*, p. 117. Decorative picture frame showing Jacopo Rubusti and his wife, Marietta, by Tintoretto (1512–1594). The pictures have been replaced with words by the present editor. See note 5.

106. Bertrand Russell, "An Outline of Intellectual Rubbish," in

Unpopular Essays (New York: Simon and Schuster, 1950), p. 110.

107. Engraved letter "T" from a design by F. Ehrmann, in *The Chefs-D'Oeuvre D'Art*, p. 64. See note vi.

108. Isabel Quigly, ed., *Shelley: Poems* (New York: Penguin Books, 1956), p. 9 and review on cover.
The Oxford Dictionary of Quotations, 3rd ed. (New York: Oxford University Press), p. 15, Matthew Arnold on Oxford.

109. The present editor takes the "inquiry" quote on faith since he was unable to confirm it in Shelley's *Philosophical View of Reform* (1819), a source given in another anthology.
Illustration of angels by Fra Sebastiano Del Piombo (1485–1547) in *The Great Painters of Christendom*, p. 99. See note 5.

110. Lucretius, *On the Nature of the Universe*, translated with introduction by R. E. Latham (New York: Penguin Classics, 1975), p. 8 and pp. 7-8, p. 92.

111. Ibid., pp. 105-106.
Santayana, "The Elements of Poetry," *Interpretations of Poetry and Religion* (1900), p. 287. See note 82.
Cicero, "On Old Age," *Selected Works*, p. 214. See note 1.

112. Lucretius, *On the Nature of the Universe*, p. 29. See note 110.

113. "Prometheus and the Ocean-Nymphs," an engraving by Kaeseberg from an original by the German artist Eduard Müller, in *Character Sketches*, vol. 3, p. 248 (facing). See note 91.

114. Lucretius, *On the Nature of the Universe*, pp. 90-91. See note 110.

115. "Thought," by H. M. A. Chapu, engraving from a statue for the tomb of Daniel Stern, the pen-name of Marie, Comtesse d'Agoult (1805-1876), a French writer and lover of Franz Liszt, the composer. *Chefs-D'Oeuvre D'Art*, p. 112 (facing). See note vi.

116. Walter Kaufmann, ed. and trans., *Twenty German Poets*, a bilingual collection (New York: Random House, Modern Library,

1962), pp. 185-187.
Huxley's remark in Francis Galton, *Memories of My Life* (London: Methuen and Co., 1908), p. 258.
Illustration: *Le Chemin Des Ecoliers* (Paris, 1861). See note 7.

117. Mark Twain, *A Horse's Tale*, illustrated by Lucius Hitchcock (New York: Harper & Brothers, 1907), p. viii.
Mark Twain, *Tom Sawyer*, afterword by George P. Elliot (New York: The New American Library Inc., 1959), p. 140 and pp. 40-41.

118. Robert N. Linscott, ed., *Selected Poems and Letters of Emily Dickinson* (New York: Doubleday Anchor Books, 1959). See review on back cover, and p. 60.

119. Ibid., p. 184.
Illustration from an article on David Neal (1838–1915) in *Modern Art and Artists* (1888). See note 41.

120. Edward S. Ellis and Charles F. Horne, *The Story of the Greatest Nations and The Worlds Famous Events*, nine volumes (New York: Francis R. Niglutsch, 1913), "The Gateway of History," frontispiece.

121. Cover of *The Colophon* (New York: The Colophon Ltd., 1931, "part six"), "a book collector's quarterly," design by T. M. Cleland.

122. Russell, "An Outline of Intellectual Rubbish," in *Unpopular Essays*, p. 106. See note 106.
Illustration from the "Cabinet of Alessandri and Son," in *The Art Journal Catalogue* (1868), p. 269. See note v.

123. "The Nightmare," by Henry Fuseli (1741–1825) in *The Great Painters of Christendom*, p. 392. See note 5.
St. Augustine, *The City of God*, edited and with an introduction by Vernon J. Bourke (New York: Doubleday, 1950), p. 176.

124. *The Portable Emerson*, new edition, edited by Carl Bode in collaboration with Malcom Cowley (New York: Viking Penguin Inc., 1981), pp. xx-xxiii, and "Compensation," p. 174; long quote on p. 167.

125. Ibid., "Fate," p. 358.
Ralph Waldo Emerson, "Swedenborg," an essay in "Represent-

ative Men," *Essays and Poems*, edited by G. F. Maine (London: Collins, 1962), pp. 369-370.

126. Emerson, "Self Reliance," in *The Portable Emerson*, pp. 162, 145, 147, 141, 148, and 151. See note 124.

127. "Fate," in *The Portable Emerson*, p. 369.
Santayana, *Interpretations of Poetry and Religion* (1900), "Emerson," pp. 217 and 219-220. See note 82.
Richard Pigot, *The Life of Man Symbolized by the Months of the Year*, illustrated by John Leighton, a young man on a ship, p. 56. See note 8.

128. Plutarch, *Lives of Noble Romans*, a selection edited by Edmund Fuller (New York: Dell Publishing Co., Inc., 1959), p. 31.
The Bible (Judges 15:15).
Plutarch, "On God's Slowness To Punish," *Essays*, translated by Robin Waterfield, introduced and annotated by Ian Kidd (New York: Penguin Books, 1992), p. 242.

129. "Samson Smiting the Philistines with the Jawbone of an Ass," an engraving by Philips Galle, after Maerten van Heemskerck, in *The Illustrated Bartsch*, vol. 56, edited by Arno Dolders (New York: Abaris Books, 1987), p. 23.

130. Livy, *The War With Hannibal*, translated by Aubrey De Selincourt and introduction by Betty Radice (New York: Penguin Books, 1975), p. 89 and pp. 510-511.

131. Xenophon, *The Persian Expedition*, translated by Rex Warner, introduction and notes by George Cawkwell (Baltimore: Penguin Books Ltd., 1972), pp. 162-163.

132. Ibid., p. 74 and introduction pp. 10 and 33.

134. Illustration from Wilfrid Meynell, ed., *Modern Art and Artists* (New York: Cassel & Co., 1888), p. 38.

135. Robert William Rogers, *Cuneiform Parallels to the Old Testament*, second edition with corrections (New York: The Abingdon Press, 1926), pp. 135-36.

136. The goddess Ishtar, painting by Edwin J. Prittie, an American artist, in *The Story of the Greatest Nations*, vol. 1, p. I-6. See note 120.

137. "Moses in the Bulrushes," by Paul Delaroche, *Great Men and Famous Women*, vol. 2, p. 2 (facing). See note 1.

138. Hume, "Of Miracles," *An Inquiry Concerning Human Understanding*, p. 130. See note 14.
See Veronica Ion, *Egyptian Mythology* (New York: The Hamlyn Publishing Group Ltd., 1968), p. 138.

139. Suetonius, *The Twelve Caesars*, translated by Robert Graves (Baltimore: Penguin Books, 1957), p. 279.

140. Illustration from *Le Chemin Des Ecoliers*, probably the goddess Venus since the woman is by a lion, p. 496. See note 7.

141. Lucretius, *On the Nature of the Universe*, translated and introduced by R. E. Latham (Baltimore: Penguin Books Ltd., 1951), pp. 77-78 and 92.

142. Voltaire, "Oedipus," act v, scene i, *The Works of Voltaire*, in forty-two volumes with a critique and biography by John Morley, various editors (New York: E. R. Dumont, 1901), vol. 16, p. 171. This version is slightly different from the one cited by Durant, *The Story of Philosophy*, p. 205.

143. "The Oracle At Delphi," painting by Henri Motte, *The Story of the Greatest Nations*, vol. 2, p. II-8. See note 120.

144. "The Questions of Zapata," in J. McCabe, ed., *Selected Works of Voltaire* (London: Watts & Co., 1921) p. 26.
Illustration of fountain showing "the Birth of Venus," by Fort from *The Art-Journal Catalogue*, p. 274. See note v.

145. "Zapata," "Question 10," and "Question 12," in McCabe, *Voltaire*, p. 27.

146. Ibid., the last question, p. 35.

147. "Tribunal of the Inquisition," a painting by A. Steinheil,

The Chefs-D'Oeuvre D'Art, description by Strahan, editor, p. 16 (facing). See note vi.

148. "The Creation of Eve," a woodcut by Albrecht Dürer, *The Illustrated Bartsch*, vol. 10, edited by Walter L. Strauss (New York: Abaris Books, 1981), p. 498.

149. John Reader, *The Rise of Life*, illustrations by John Gurche, (New York: Alfred A. Knopf, 1986), detail of "The Tower of Time" with the face of a Neanderthal man lit by firelight, p. 153.

150. "Zapata," in McCabe, *Voltaire*, "Question 13," p. 27. See note 144.

151. "The Deluge," by Melchior Lorck in *The German Single-Leaf Woodcut* (1550–1600), vol. 2, p. 602. See note 89.

152. "Adam and Eve Seduced by the Demon," by an anonymous Italian artist of the sixteenth century in *The Illustrated Bartsch*, vol. 33 (formerly vol. 16, part II), edited by Henri Zerner (New York: Abaris Books, 1979), p. 280.

153. "The Professor and His Pupil," engraving from a painting by John Bagnold Burgess (late 19th-century British painter) in *The Treasury of Art* (1883), p. 136. See note 32.

154. "Buoyant Doubt," in Louis Untermeyer, *Modern American Poetry: A Critical Anthology*, 5th edition (New York: Harcourt, Brace and Company, 1936), p. 347.

155. George Santayana, *Scepticism and Animal Faith* (New York: Dover Publications, Inc., 1923, reprinted 1955), p. 69.
Engraving of a work in "Terra-Cotta" of "high Art," manufactured by Herren March, of Charlottensburg, Berlin from *The Art-Journal Catalogue*, p. 220. See note v.

156. *The Oxford Dictionary of Quotations*, p. 108. See note 92.
Fawn Brodie, *The Devil Drives: A Life of Sir Richard Burton* (New York: W. W. Norton and Company, 1967), biography on cover.

157. Ibid., p. 141, Burton's journal entry, December 2, 1856.
"Aurora," by Guercino (Giovanni Francesco Barbieri: 1592-

1666), *The Great Painters of Christendom*, p 145. See note 5.

158. True Williams, *Frank Fairweather's Fortunes*, illustrated by the author (Juvenile Book House, copyright 1895 by Robert O. Law), frontispiece.

159. Daniel Defoe, *The Life and Strange Surprising Adventures of Robinson Crusoe of York, Mariner*, illustrations by "The Brothers Louis and Frederick RHEAD" (New York: R. H. Russell, 1900), p. 1.

160. Merrill D. Peterson, ed., *Thomas Jefferson: Writings* (New York: The Library of America, 1984), p. 1430.
For a slightly edited reprint of Jefferson's letter to William Short (October 31, 1819), see Merrill D. Peterson, ed., *The Portable Thomas Jefferson* (The Viking Press, New York, 1975), p. 564. Jefferson's letter (Paris, August 10, 1787) to his nephew Peter Carr, is also in the same volume, p. 425.

161. The Bible (John 8:1-9 and Matthew 7:1).

162. Eric Hoffer, *The True Believer* (New York: Harper & Row, Publishers, 1951), cover and p. 81.

163. Ibid., p. 77.
Design from an article on Abraham Bloemaert (1564–1651), in *The Great Painters of Christendom*, p. 200. See note 5.

164. Isabel Quigly, ed., *Shelley: Poems*, (New York: Penguin Books, 1956), review on cover, and p. 9. See note 108.
"Alastor; or Spirit of Solitude," lines 689-690, *John Keats and Percy Bysshe Shelley: Complete Poetical Works*, with notes by Mrs. Shelley (New York: Random House, Inc., undated), p. 19.
Untermeyer, *A Concise Treasury of Great Poems*, commentary on Shelley, p. 250. See note 60.

165. "Prometheus Unbound," act iv, lines 570-578, *John Keats and Percy Bysshe Shelley: Complete Poetical Works*, p. 293.

166. John Tyndall, "Apology for the Belfast Address," *Fragments of Science for Unscientific People* (New York: A. L. Burt, Publisher, 1880?), pp. 501, 472, and footnote on p. 473.

167. Tyndall, "Science and Man," *Fragments of Science*, p. 622.

Tyndall spoke of "the Abraham of scientific men," but the present editor has used the more eloquent paraphrase, quoted by H. L. Mencken in A New Dictionary of Quotations, p. 252—"the Abraham of science."

Francis Darwin, ed., The Life and Letters of Charles Darwin (New York: D. Appleton and Company, 1898), vol. 1, p. 274 and p. 282. Darwin's reply in 1879 to a letter by Rev. J. Fordyce.

168. Tyndall, "Apology for the Belfast Address" (1874), in Fragments, p. 501. See note 166.

169. "The Creation of the Fish and Birds," in Masterpieces from the works of Gustave Doré, by Edmund Ollier (New York: Cassell & Company, Limited, 1887), unpaged volume.

170. Untermeyer, A Concise Treasury of Great Poems, on W. E. Henley, pp. 379-380. See note 60.

Letter design by Ehrmann, in The Chefs-D'Oeuvre D'Art, a man with a torch, p. 60. See note vi.

171. The Viking Book of Poetry of the English-Speaking World, vol. 2, pp. 1067-1068, where Henley's poem is listed as "I.M." "R.T. Hamilton Bruce." See note 101.

172. Richard Lovelace, "To Althea from Prison," in A Concise Treasury of Great Poems, pp. 140-141. See note 60.

173. "Grief of the Oceanides at the Fate of Prometheus," by Charles Lehmann (1814–1882) in The Masterpieces of German Art, p. 28 (facing, next page). See note 87.

Ernest Hemingway, The Old Man and the Sea (New York: Charles Scribner's Sons, 1952), pp. 66 and 103.

174. Wording added to unidentified design in The Great Painters of Christendom (1877), from an article about Hubert Van Eyck (c. 1366–1426) and John Van Eyck (c. 1390–1441), founders of the Flemish school of painting, p. 156. See note 5.

175. Engraving of lady raising a lamp to the world from Barnes' Complete Geography (New York: A. S. Barnes and Company, 1885), frontispiece. Artist not identified.

Voltaire, Essai sur les Moeurs, introduction. Quoted from

Durant, The Story of Philosophy, p. 220. See note 12.

176. Faust (First Part), translated by Peter Salm (New York: Bantam Books, 1885), p. 105, lines 1699-1702, and p. xv.
"The greatest German of all time." Walter Kaufmann, trans., Goethe's Faust (New York: Doubleday & Company, 1961), p. 3.

177. E. D. Pendry, ed., Christopher Marlowe, Complete Plays and Poems, textual adviser, J. C. Maxwell (London: J. M. Dent & Sons, 1976), p. 326, Doctor Faustus, act v, scene ii, lines 190-191.
Walter Kaufmann, trans., Goethe's Faust, "The Second Part of the Tragedy," p. 493 (lines 11,936-11,937) and p. 469 (lines 11,573-11,576). See note 176.

178. Ibid., p. 253, lines 2557-2565, and p. 275, lines 2836-2840.

179. "Mephistopheles and Faust," by A. Jacomin, Character Sketches, vol. 3, p. 40 (facing). See note 91.

180. Goethe, Faust, unidentified translation found in The Philosophy of Humanism, by Corliss Lamont (New York: Fredrick Ungar Press, 1965), p. 193. Lamont's book is so thoroughly footnoted that one "off-the-cuff" quotation may be forgiven.
"Illustration" header, The Treasury of Art (1886), p. vii. See note 32.

181. Rubaiyat of Omar Khayyam, rendered into English verse by Edward Fitzgerald, with illustrations by Edmund Dulac (New York: Garden City Books, New York, 1952), quatrain lxvi, p. 112, cover biography by an unnamed editor.
The Great Painters of Christendom, illustration with an article on Simon Vouet, a French painter, p. 287. See note 5.

182. Santayana, Reason in Common Sense, p. 176. See note 5.
Illustration from Le Chemin Des Ecoliers, p. 188. See note 7.

183. Santayana, Reason in Common Sense, p. 201. See note 5.
Design from Modern Art and Artists, p. 81. See note 41.

184. Huxley's letter to Charles Kingsley, Sept. 23, 1860, in Leonard Huxley, Life and Letters of Thomas Henry Huxley, (New York: D. Appleton and Company, 1909), vol. 1, p. 237.

185. Miriam Allott, ed., *The Poems of Matthew Arnold*, 2nd ed. (New York: Longman, 1979), p. 181 (scene ii, act i, lines 397-402, from "Empedocles on Etna").
Illustration of sea from *The Poetical Works of Henry Wadsworth Longfellow* (1880), vol. 2, p. 247. See note 9.

186. "On the Relations of Man to the Lower Animals," an essay in Huxley's *Man's Place in Nature* (New York: Greenwood Press, Publishers, 1968, originally published by D. Appleton & Co., London, 1896), pp. 154-155.

187. "The Mountain Sprite," an engraving from a painting by Conrad Dielitz, *The Treasury of Art* (1883), p. 344. See note 32.

188. Sir Paul Harvey, ed., *The Oxford Companion to English Literature*, p. 177, on Arthur Hugh Clough. See note 60.
See also commentary on Clough by L. Untermeyer, *A Concise Treasury of Great Poems*, p. 331. See note 60.
Letter "A" from *The Treasury of Art* (1883), showing Perseus rescuing Andreomeda, who had been chained to a rock to appease Poseidon, the sea god. See note 32.

189. *A Concise Treasury of Great Poems*, p. 332.

190. Henry David Thoreau, *Walden, or Life in the Woods and On the Duty of Civil Disobedience* (New York: Harper and Row, Publishers, 1965), p. 83.
The Oxford Companion to English Literature, p. 817. See note 60.

191. "A Summer Evening," by "Mr. Hennessy," *Modern Art and Artists*, p. 125. See note 41.

192. "Washing Venus," from a painting by Carl Gussow (1843-1907), *The Masterpieces of German Art*, vol. 1, p. 83. See note 87.

193. "Fruitless Labor," an engraving after Rudolf Geyling (b. 1840), *Masterpieces of German Art*, p. 53.

194. E. G. Sandford, *Memoirs of Archbishop Temple by Seven Friends* (New York: Macmillan and Company, 1906), vol. 2, p. 705.
"A Good Story," by Leo-Hermann, *The Masterpieces of French Art*, vol. 2, no page numbers in first half. See note 85.

195. Letter "C," by an unnamed artist accompanying an engraving of "The Reception by Richelieu," by Adrien Moreau in *The Masterpieces of French Art*, vol. 2, unpaged section. See note 85.

196. *The Complete Poems of Keats and Shelley*, Keats, "Endymion," book I, line 1, p. 47; "On the Grasshopper and Cricket," line 1, p. 33; "Ode to a Nightingale," stanza iv, p. 184; "Ode on a Grecian Urn," stanza v, p. 186. See note 164.

197. *The Complete Poems of Keats and Shelley*, Keats, "The Fall of Hyperion, A Dream" (1819), canto i, lines 1-2, p. 353.
The Life of Man Symbolized by the Months of the Year (London, 1866), a man chasing tomorrow, p. 139. See note 8.
Hanging men from *Le Chemin des Ecoliers* (Paris, 1861). See note 7.

198. *The Complete Poems of Keats and Shelley*, Keats, "The Fall of Hyperion, A Dream," lines 19-31, p. 353.

199. "Iphigenia," by artist Edmund Kanoldt, *Character Sketches*, vol. 2, facing p. 214. See note 91.

200. Jack London, *The People of the Abyss* (California: Joseph Simon Publisher, Sonoma State University, 1980), pp. vii, 140, and 147. Engraved letter from *Chefs-D'Oeuvre D'Art*. See note vi.

201. J. London, *The People of the Abyss*, p. xv.

202. "The Absence of Religion in Shakespeare," an essay in Santayana's *Interpretations of Poetry and Religion*, p. 152. See note 82.
Illustration from a work by Eugene Fromentin (1820–1876), in *The Chefs-D'Oeuvre D'Art*, a procession, p. 72. See note vi.

203. Santayana, "The Absence of Religion in Shakespeare," pp. 153 and 161.

204. *A Truthtelling Manual and the Art of Worldly Wisdom*, a collection of the aphorisms from the works of Baltasar Gracian, translated by Martin Fischer from a 1653 text (Baltimore, Md: Charles C. Thomas, 1934), pp. 147, 267, and 172.

205. Ibid., p. 32.
Clock design by M. Noel Guillet, in *The Art-Journal Catalogue*,

p. 298. See note v.

206. Prescott, *History of the Conquest of Mexico* (Modern Library edition), p. 157, 694, 427, and 627. See note 102.

207. Bernal Diaz del Castillo, *The True History of the Conquest of Mexico* (first draft, 1568, reprinted by Readex Microprint Corporation, location not given, 1966), pp. 130-131.

208. Aristotle, *On Man in the Universe*, edited by Louise Ropes Loomis (New York: Classics Club, Walter J. Black, Inc, Roslyn, 1943), pp. xxxvi, xiii, and xxxvii (introduction).

209. Ibid., p. 107, "Nicomachean Ethics."
Illustration: "My Writing-Table," by Annie Brassey in her article on "The Decoration of a Yacht" in *The Treasury of Art* (1883). See note 32.

210. Aristotle, *On Man in the Universe*, pp. 283-284, "Politics."
Illustration: Unidentified painting by Jean-Francis de Troy (1679-1752) in *The Great Painters of Christendom*. See note 5.

211. "Reconciliation," design by Walter Crane, in *The Treasury of Art* (1886), p. 453. See note 32.

212. *Poems of Edwin Markham*, selected and arranged by Charles L. Wallis (New York: Harper & Brothers, Publishers, 1950), p. 3.
Santayana, *Interpretations of Poetry and Religion* (1900), p. 287. See note 82.

213. "The French School," design by unnamed artist, wording replaced with "Philosophy Perennis," *The Great Painters of Christendom*, p. 281. See note 5.

214. Untermeyer, *A Concise Treasury of Great Poems*, commentary on William Blake, pp. 186-187. See note 60.

215. "Auguries of Innocence," *The Portable Blake*, edited by Alfred Kazin (New York: Penguin Books, 1974), p. 150. Commentary quoted from Kazin's introduction, pp. 10-11.
See also *The Top 500 Poems*, edited by William Harmon (New York: Columbia University Press, 1992), p. 382.

216. Sophocles, *Antigone*, chorus, second ode, *The Three Tragedies: Antigone, Oedipus the King and Electra*, translated by H. D. F. Kitto (New York: Oxford University Press, 1964), p. 13. Translation slightly different from the one used in the present volume.
Vase by MM. Duron, *The Art-Journal Catalogue*, p. 227. See note v.

217. True Williams, *Frank Fairweather's Fortunes*, illustrated by author (New York [?]: Juvenile Book House, 1895), p. 366.

218. Camille Flammarion, *Popular Astronomy: A General Description of the Heavens*, translated by J. Ellard Gore (New York: D. Appleton and Company, 1894), p. 109.

219. I. Quigley, ed., *Shelley: Poems*, p. 107. See note 108.

220. *The Advancement of Learning*, vol. 5 of book 8, *The Works of Francis Bacon*, chapter 2, p. 78. See note 12.
Santayana, *Reason in Religion*, vol. 3 of *The Life of Reason*, pp. 3-4. See note 5.
Illustration: Figure from "The Cabinet of Alessandri and Son," *The Art Journal Catalogue*. See note v.

221. "The Castle," in *The Classic and the Beautiful from the Literature of Three Thousand Years*, edited by Henry Coppee (Philadelphia: Carson & Simpson, 1891), vol. 3, p. 442 (facing). Artist identified only as "Devereux."

222. P. Harvey, ed., *The Oxford Companion to English Literature*, commentary on Wordsworth, pp. 898-899. See note 60.
L. Untermeyer, *A Concise Treasury of Great Poems*, commentary on Wordsworth, p. 202 and p. 210. See note 60.
Illustration from *Le Chemin Des Ecoliers* (Paris, 1861), p. 175. See note 7.

223. Wordsworth, "My Heart Leaps Up," *The Viking Book of Poetry of the English-Speaking World*, vol. 2, p. 655. See note 171.

224. See H. Rider Haggard, *King Solomon's Mines* (Pyramid Books, New York, 1966). A wonderful story!
Illustration from *Le Chemin Des Ecoliers* (Paris, 1861), p. 2. See note 7.

225. "Requiem," in *The Viking Book of Poetry of the English-Speaking World*, vol. 2, pp. 1071-1072. See note 171.

226. Robert Louis Stevenson, "Envoy," from "Underwoods," *An Inland Voyage* (1878), edition with the frontispiece of Pan (New York: The Co-operative Publication Society, 1904), p. 17.

227. Ibid., frontspiece.
Edith Hamilton, *Mythology: Timeless Tales of Gods and Heroes* (New York: New American Library, 1940), p. 40.

228. "Satyr and Nymphs," by William Bouguereau in *Selected Pictures*, vol. 2, facing p. 88. See note 25.

229. Mark Twain, *Roughing It*, with a foreword by Leonard Kriegel (New York: New American Library, 1962, originally 1872), p. 105.

230. "The People, Yes" (1936), a poem of some 180 pages, each page sprinkled with gems, in *The Complete Poems of Carl Sandburg*, revised and expanded edition, introduction by Archibald MacLeish (Harcourt Brace Jovanovich, Inc., 1969), part 64, p. 539.
Martin Gardner, *Fads and Fallacies in the Name of Science* (New York: Dover, 1956).

231. The last lines of "The People, Yes," *The Complete Poems of Carl Sandburg*, part 107, p. 617.

232. L. Huxley, *Life and Letters of Thomas Henry Huxley*, vol. 1, pp. 197-199. See note 184.

233. Ibid., p. 199.
Illustration from *The Great Painters of Christendom* in an article about Ghirlandaio (1449–1498). See note 5.

234. Jerome Nathanson, "Sixty-six Million Americans Do Not Belong to Any Church: What Do They Believe?" *Religions in America*, edited by Leo Rosten (New York: Simon and Schuster, 1963), p. 217-218. Unfortunately, Nathanson's article was dropped from later editions of Rosten's book.
Eusebius quoted in Gilbert Murray, *Five Stages of Greek Religion* (Garden City, N.Y.: Doubleday & Company, 1951), pp. 188-189.

235. "At A Child's Grave," Washington, D. C. (January 8, 1882), in *The Works of Robert G. Ingersoll*, vol. 12, p. 399. See note 19.

"Geni Guarding the Secret of the Tomb," sculpture by Rene de Saint-Marceaux, in *The Masterpieces of French Art* (1882?), vol. 2, unpaged. See note 85.

236. Data on the Puritans from Robert M. Adams, *Ben Jonson's Plays and Masques* (New York: W. W. Norton & Company, 1979), p. 482. *The Alchemist*, act v, scene 1, p. 258. See the fascinating notes on pages 9, 123, 211, 218, 220, and 258.

237. Ben Jonson, *Underwoods* (1616), "Oak and Lily," in Untermeyer, *A Concise Treasury of Great Poems*, p. 97. See note 60.

A girl in a swing, by Pierre-Marie Beyle, *Selected Pictures*, vol. 2, p. 90. See note 25.

238. Untermeyer, *A Concise Treasury of Great Poems*, p. 96. *Oxford Companion to English Literature*, p. 437. See note 60.

Seganus, in *The complete Plays of Ben Jonson*, edited by G.A. Wilkes (London: Clarion Press, 1981), p. 264.

239. "The indiscreet soubrette," an engraving after a work by Jules Emile Saintin, *The Chefs-D'Oeuvre D'Art*, p. 130 (facing). See note vi.

240. Edith Hamilton, *The Greek Way*, with an introduction by C. M. Bowra (New York: W.W. Norton & Company, Inc, 1930— reprinted by Time-Life Books, Inc., New York, 1963), pp. ix, x, xvii, and xxii.

241. Ibid., pp. 10-11.

Illustration from *The Treasury of Art* (1886), p. vi (Introduction). See note 32.

242. Hamilton, *The Greek Way*, pp. xxi-xxii. See note 240.

243. Engraved letter "N" from a design by F. Ehrmann in *The Chefs-D'Oeuvre D'Art*, p. 8. See note vi.

244. Cicero, *The Nature of the Gods*, introduction by J. M. Ross, translated by Horace C. P. McGregor (New York: Penguin Books, 1972), p. 61. See Voltaire, *Philosophical Dictionary*, under "Cicero."

Cicero, "On Old Age," *Selected Works*, translated with introduction by Michael Grant, p. 247. See note 1.

Cicero, *On the Good Life*, translated with introduction by Michael Grant (New York: Penguin Books, 1971), p. 7, 117.

245. Cicero, "On the State", III, parts 23, 33. See introduction in *Selected Works*, translated Michael Grant, p. 7-8. See note 1.

See alternative translation in Cicero, *On the Commonwealth* (Ohio State University Press, Columbus, Ohio, 1929), pp. 215-216.

Plato, *The Republic*, book viii, and Plato, *The Apology*. Translations from another anthology but not identified.

246. Cicero, "Discussions at Tusculum," *On the Good Life*, trans. Michael Grant, p. 105. See note 244.

Jacob Bronowski, *The Ascent of Man* (Boston: Little, Brown and Company, 1973), p. 427.

247. Cicero, "On Old Age," *Selected Works*, p. 214. See note 244.

Unidentified engraving after a work by Sebastian Bourdon (1616–1671), *The Great Painters of Christendom*. See note 5.

248. Giorgio de Santillana, *The Crime of Galileo* (Chicago, Ill.: University of Chicago Press, 1955), p. 98.

Martin Gardner, "Geology versus Genesis," in *Fads and Fallacies in the Name of Science* (New York: Dover Publications, Inc., 1957), p. 137.

249. Santillana, *The Crime of Galileo*, pp. 97-98, Galileo's "Letter to the Grand Duchess Cristina of Lorraine." Santillana's less-eloquent translation goes, "the most pernicious possible way for the souls of men...convincing themselves of the truth of an opinion which it was a sin to believe." Present translation not located.

Goethe's Faust, translated by Walter Kaufmann, p. 195, lines 1856-1854. See note 176.

Figure from the "Cabinet of Alessandri and Son," *The Art-Journal Catalogue*, p. 269. See note v.

250. *Marcus Aurelius and His Times*, with an introduction by Irwin Edman, translated by George Long (Roslyn, NY: The Classics Club, Walter J. Black, Inc., 1945), pp. 48, 98, 25, 97, 126, 36, and 37 (footnote), 33, 124.

251. Engraved letter "S," in *The Chefs-D'Oeuvre D'Art*, p. 12. See

note vi.
Marcus Aurelius, *Meditations*, in *Marcus Aurelius and His Times*, p. 31.

252. Henry Beston, *The Outermost House: A Year of Life on the Great Beach of Cape Cod* (New York: The Viking Press, 1928), p. 176. E. Hamilton, *The Greek Way*, p. xxiii. See note 240.

253. "A Voyage to the Moon," by Gustave Doré as an illustration for *Baron Munchausen, Narrative of his Marvellous Travels* (1758), by Rudolph Erich Raspe, in *Masterpieces from the Works of Gustave Doré*, edited by E. Ollier.

254. *Rubaiyat of Omar Khayyam*, quatrain xii. See note 181.

255. "Lalla Rookh," engraved by W. Edwards after a work by A. de Valentine, *Character Sketches*, vol. 2, p. 292 (facing). See note 91.

256. Matthew Arnold, *Culture and Anarchy* (Ann Arbor: University of Michigan Press, 1965, reprint of the 1869 edition), p. 88.
Illustration: from an article about Angelica Kauffmann, in *The Great Painters of Christendom*, p. 264. See note 5.

257. "Dover Beach," in *Matthew Arnold: Selected Poems and Prose*, edited, with introduction and notes by Miriam Allott (London: J. M. Dent & Sons Ltd., 1978), pp. 88–89.

258. Goethe, *Wilhelm Meister's Apprenticeship*, edited and translated by Eric A. Blackall in cooperation with Victor Lange (New York: Suhrkamp Publishers, 1983), book 3, chapter 1, heading.

259. "Alexis and Dora," engraving by C. Preisel after a work by W. von Kaulbach, in *Character Sketches*, vol. 1, p. 26 (facing). See note 91.

260. Benjamin Disraeli, *Endymion* (New York: M. Walter Dunne, 1904, AMS Press Inc., reprint, 1976), vol. 2, p. 129.

261. "En Rout," illustration (artist not identified) for a poem by Tennyson, in *Gems of Poetry*, edited by Richard S. Rhodes (Chicago: Rhodes & McClure Publishing Co., 1885), p. 17 (facing).

262. "Hamlet," act ii, scene ii, *The Portable Shakespeare* (New

York: The Viking Press, 1965), p. 46.

263. "Gloria Victis," from a sculpture by Marius Jean Antonin, in *The Chefs-D'Oeuvre D'Art*, p. 20 (facing). See note vi.

264. Michael Frayn (1933–), a British novelist and playwright, quoted by Paul Theroux in *The Great Railway Bazaar* (1975).

265. "Time Sustaining Truth," by Nicolas Poussin, in *The Treasury of Art* (1886), p. 152. See note 32.

266. An early partial statement of the "Humanist Credo" is found in "Six Interviews on Talmage" (1882), in which Robert Ingersoll said: "My creed is this . . . ." *The Works of Robert Ingersoll*, vol. 5, pp. 20-21. See note 19.
Lamont, *The Philosophy of Humanism*, p. 73. See note 180.

267. "Time Bringing Truth to Light," engraving by Philips Galle, after a work by Federico Zuccaro, in *The Illustrated Bartsch*, vol. 56, *Netherlandish Artists*, edited by Arno Dolders, (New York: Abaris Books, 1987), p. 311.

268. The "Finis" design from *The Art-Journal Catalogue*, p. 331. See note v.

INDEX